NELSON EDUCATION SERIES
IN HUMAN RESOURCES MANAGEMENT

FOURTH EDITION

Strategic Compensation

A Simulation

Richard J. Long

EDWARDS SCHOOL OF BUSINESS

UNIVERSITY OF SASKATCHEWAN

Henry S. Ravichander

EDWARDS SCHOOL OF BUSINESS

UNIVERSITY OF SASKATCHEWAN

NELSON EDUCATION

NELSON / EDUCATION

**Strategic Compensation: A Simulation,
Fourth Edition**

by Richard J. Long, Henry S. Ravichander

**Associate Vice President,
Editorial Director:**
Evelyn Veitch

**Editor-in-Chief,
Higher Education:**
Anne Williams

Acquisitions Editor:
Amie Plourde

Marketing Manager:
Kathaleen McCormick

Developmental Editor:
Jenny O'Reilly

Senior Content Production Manager:
Imoinda Romain

Proofreader:
Carrie McGregor

Manufacturing Manager:
Joanne McNeil

Cover Design:
Martyn Schmoll

Cover Image:
urbancow/iStockphoto

Printer:
Webcom

Table of Contents

About the Authors

Richard J. Long is Professor and Head of the Department of Human Resources and Organizational Behaviour at the Edwards School of Business of the University of Saskatchewan. He holds B.Com and MBA degrees from the University of Alberta, and a Ph.D. from Cornell University in New York, and is a Certified Human Resources Professional (CHRP). Dr. Long has been teaching, conducting research, and consulting on human resources management for more than thirty years, and has produced more than one hundred publications based on his research and experience. He is currently on the editorial boards of *The International Journal of Human Resource Management* and *Relations Industrielles/Industrial Relations*. He is the author of *Strategic Compensation in Canada*, the leading compensation text in Canada, the fourth edition of which was published by Nelson Education in 2010. It is the companion textbook to this simulation.

Henry S. Ravichander (Ravi) has been a Sessional Lecturer at the Edwards School of Business of the University of Saskatchewan since 1998, teaching courses in organizational behaviour, business policy, marketing, and management skills. He holds an MBA from the University of Saskatchewan, and undergraduate degrees from Indiana-Purdue University and Bangalore University. Prior to his MBA, he worked for the Arabian American Oil Company for many years as a planning analyst.

Preface

More than ever, having the right compensation system can mean the difference between a company's success and its failure. However, identifying the right compensation system for a given firm is no easy matter, since a system that works well for one firm could be a disaster for another. And even if a firm does correctly identify the compensation strategy that will add the most value to that firm, the process of converting that strategy into a successfully operating compensation system is a long and arduous one, fraught with many difficulties and pitfalls along the way.

Used in conjunction with a text that provides a conceptual framework for identifying and designing the compensation system that best fits a given organization, this simulation provides an opportunity for students to enrich their understanding of the compensation process by applying these concepts to a simulated organization. In so doing, they will design a compensation system from start to finish, from strategy to implementation.

During this process, student teams will grapple with a wide array of compensation issues and problems, which include identifying the right compensation strategy, designing job evaluation and pay-for-knowledge systems, identifying actual market values, designing performance pay and benefits plans, and applying the system to "real-life" employees, to name just some.

Most students find this a very intensive and challenging experience, but most also find that this approach provides a much stronger connection between concept and reality than they normally encounter during their educational careers. When they are finished, most students report that by actually applying the conceptual material, they have learned much more than otherwise possible, and that what they have learned sticks with them much better. They also gain practical skills that employers value.

Although it could also be used in conjunction with any text that provides a comprehensive framework for designing compensation systems, this simulation has been designed to accompany Richard Long's text, *Strategic Compensation in Canada*, fourth edition, published by Nelson Education in 2010. As with the third edition, the fourth edition of *Strategic Compensation in Canada* has been designed so that the simulation and the text serve as complements to one another.

The fourth edition of the simulation has been revised in several ways. The case information has been updated, as has the market data and employee compensation data in the software (CompSoft). CompSoft has also been modified to make it more user-friendly. The instructors' notes package has been revised accordingly.

The authors have found feedback from earlier users very useful, and welcome any suggestions or comments you may wish to provide. We can be contacted by email (long@edwards.usask.ca), fax (306-966-2514), telephone (306-966-8398), or postal mail (Edwards School of Business, University of Saskatchewan, Saskatoon, S7N 5A7). We look forward to hearing from you!

Acknowledgements

The authors would like to convey their appreciation to the many people who played a role in bringing this project to fruition. First and foremost, we would like to thank our students, whose desire to more deeply understand all sorts of human resource issues, including compensation, motivated this project. We would like to extend special thanks to those students in our compensation classes whose feedback allowed us to smooth out the rough edges in earlier versions of this simulation. Special thanks are also due to Marnie Polansky, who assisted this project in a variety of ways. We would like to thank the reviewers commissioned by Nelson for their feedback, as well as Monica Belcourt, editor for the Nelson Series in Human Resources Management, and the team at Nelson, including Evelyn Veitch and Jenny O'Reilly. Finally, we owe our deepest debt to our families, without whose encouragement and love this project could not have been completed.

Your Challenge

The Scenario

You are a top-notch team of compensation professionals employed at a leading compensation consulting firm. Your team is so highly respected that two of your company's major clients, Duplox Copiers Canada Limited and Zenith Medical Systems Incorporated, are vying for your services. However, because of all your commitments, you will be able to take on only one of these clients, so one of them will be out of luck. Your boss is in the process of deciding which client will get your services, and will give you a decision shortly.

Your Mission

Your mission is to analyze your client firm, identify the sources of the problems the firm is facing, recommend any necessary organizational changes, formulate a new reward and compensation strategy, and design and implement a compensation system that will maximize your client's success. Due to the magnitude of your task, you will complete this project in three phases. At the end of each phase you will submit a report to your client, and give a brief presentation describing your analysis and key recommendations to that point.

In Phase I, you will analyze the current organizational system, identify problems and their causes, propose solutions, outline an effective reward and compensation strategy, develop and apply a job evaluation system for some jobs, and develop a pay-for-knowledge system for other jobs. (Your client has seen pay-for-knowledge plans at other organizations and wants to try one, but only wants to apply it to a limited number of jobs to see how it might work at their company.) Currently, your client firm does not use either job evaluation or pay for knowledge, and simply relies on a rather haphazard form of market pricing.

Phase II will involve calibrating your compensation system to the market, applying market data to the pay structures that flow from your compensation strategy, job evaluation system, and pay-for-knowledge plan. The result of Phase II will be a pay structure that provides a pay range for every job at your client firm, including the actual dollar values for base pay, performance pay, and indirect pay that will be provided for each job.

Phase III will involve operationalizing the new compensation system, by fleshing out your performance pay and indirect pay plans, by adjusting compensation of current employees into your new system, and by developing procedures for the implementation and ongoing management of your compensation system.

Your Learning Objectives

The best way of mastering any body of knowledge is to apply it in a real-life setting. But when that is not possible, the next best thing can be a simulated reality. The purpose of this simulation is to provide a vehicle through which you can apply your compensation knowledge, acquired from your text and your classes, to enrich your learning about this crucial topic.

You will find this project challenging. It requires a lot of hard thinking and a lot of hard work. In fact, most students say that it is the toughest thing they have done in their student careers. On the other hand, most also say that they learned a lot more than in other courses, and that what they learned has stuck with them. Most students enjoy being able to merge theory with practice, and take away a set of skills that can be immediately applied outside of their student lives. Students also enjoy finding that many employers value these skills enough to hire them in preference to someone without these skills! Of course, compensation knowledge is an integral part of the requirements for becoming a Certified Human Resources Professional (CHRP), which also helps career progress.

By the time you finish this compensation simulation, you will understand the compensation process from beginning to end, from strategy to practice. You will be able to:

- Identify the problems that can be caused by an ineffective compensation system.

- Understand how the compensation system and other structural and strategic variables intertwine.

- Identify the compensation strategy that best fits a given firm.

- Design effective job evaluation and pay-for-knowledge systems.

- Design effective performance pay plans and benefits systems.

- Utilize market data to calibrate the compensation structure.

- Design effective processes for compensation system implementation and ongoing management.

- Explain why compensation system change is so difficult, and how to increase odds for success.

Duplox Copiers Canada Limited

Your Client

Your client is Duplox Copiers Canada Limited, a wholly owned subsidiary of Duplox Copiers Incorporated, which is a large multi-national firm based in the United States. Duplox Copiers Canada Limited (DCCL) is responsible for the sales, installation, and servicing of Duplox-brand copiers, but not for their manufacturing, which is carried out in other countries. DCCL has about 1,200 employees, most of them located in branch offices across Canada.

The head office for Duplox Canada is located in Toronto, and Chart 1 shows the organization structure at head office. The executive committee consists of the CEO and the two vice presidents. The company has six departments – marketing, finance & administration, human resources, inventory management, technical services, and technical training and support.

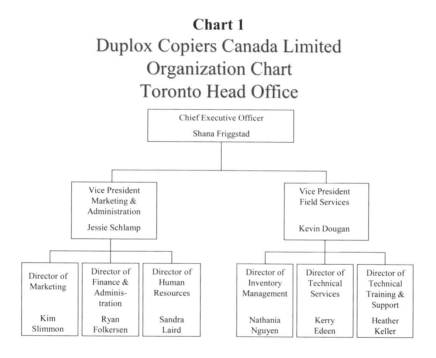

Chart 1
Duplox Copiers Canada Limited
Organization Chart
Toronto Head Office

Shana Friggstad, the President and Chief Executive Officer of Duplox Copiers Canada Limited, has requested your consulting services, and is delighted that your team was assigned to her firm. DCCL is experiencing serious performance problems: employee turnover is up and morale is down; customer satisfaction is down and complaints are up; and, most importantly, revenue and profits are both down. President Friggstad knows that the compensation system used by a firm can contribute to all these problems, and since compensation is a major cost item for her firm (currently accounting for about 44% of the firm's costs) she suspects that the firm's compensation system may be implicated in these problems. But she can't be sure without your help.

Because President Friggstad recognizes that compensation is just one of several important structural variables that must all fit together if effective organizational performance is to occur, you are authorized to suggest any changes to the managerial strategy and structure of the organization that needed to make the new compensation system work. Your only limitation is that she wants no changes made to the company's six-department structure, which she believes is the best way to organize. Beyond that, you have free rein to make recommendations about reward structure, job design, and the other structural dimensions.

Duplox Operations and Structure

DCCL earns revenues in three main ways. First, through the margin on the sale of copiers. The U.S. parent company sets the prices that Duplox Canada must pay for the copiers, but allows Duplox Canada to charge whatever price the market will bear. Second, DCCL is reimbursed by the parent company for work that is covered by the manufacturer's warranty. This aspect of the business is not very profitable, since the parent company is not very generous in its reimbursement levels. Third, DCCL sells service contracts on the equipment that customers purchase. This is a very significant source of company revenues, and is directly dependent on the quality of service provided.

A major problem in recent years is that the company's technical service specialists (TSSs) appear to be experiencing declining attitudes toward their work and the company, as indicated by the firm's annual attitude survey and increased turnover, and there has been a sharp increase in customer complaints about machine breakdowns and the quality of service received. TSSs install new machines, provide scheduled maintenance at regular intervals, and provide emergency maintenance in case of breakdowns, malfunctions, or copy quality problems.

The performance of the technical service specialists is crucial to customer satisfaction with company products. Indeed, the Director of Marketing has been complaining bitterly that "poor performance of the service personnel is crippling the efforts of my sales force." The Director of Technical Services bitterly resents this criticism, believing that his department deserves praise, not criticism, for its productivity improvement and cost cutting during the past two years—where the same number of machines are now being serviced by 20% fewer TSSs.

Duplox Canada employs about 550 technical service specialists located at about 25 branch offices across Canada. The operations of the company are divided into five geographical regions, each with about five branch offices. The Prairies (covering Alberta, Saskatchewan, and Manitoba) is one such region, and there are branch offices in Calgary (where the Regional Sales and Service Managers are also located), Edmonton, Saskatoon, Regina, and Winnipeg. Charts 2 and 3 show the structure of the Technical Services Department, and the structure of the Edmonton Branch, which is a typical branch office.

Chart 2

Duplox Copiers Canada Limited
Technical Services Department

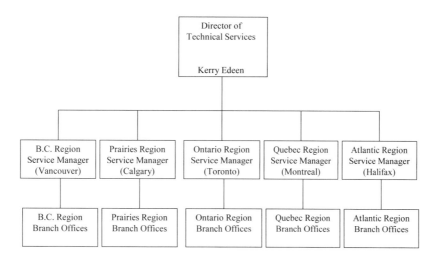

Chart 3

Technical Services Department
Edmonton Branch
Service Section

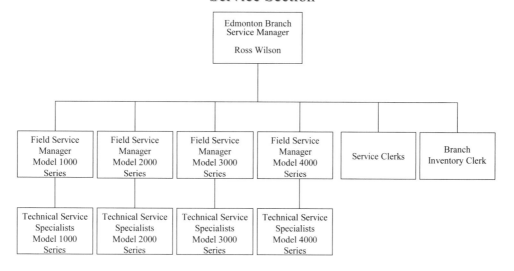

The Edmonton Branch has about 22 TSSs, and is responsible for the northern half of Alberta. The branch is co-managed by a branch service manager and branch sales manager. The branch sales manager supervises approximately eight sales representatives, along with an office manager, who supervises two clerical staff. (Overall, Duplox employs about 200 sales reps across Canada.) The branch sales manager reports to a regional sales manager based in Calgary, who reports to the Director of Marketing in Toronto. Charts 4 and 5 illustrate reporting relationships in the Marketing Department.

The branch service manager supervises a small parts warehouse at the branch (most parts are kept at the national warehouse in Toronto to reduce inventory costs), a couple of service clerks, and four Field Service Managers (FSMs), each of whom supervises five or six technical service specialists. Because of an increasing variety and complexity of machines, each FSM and the TSSs under them specialize in a particular category of machine. Each FSM handles the scheduling of service and installation of all machines in their category (e.g., the model 1000 series, which includes a variety of smaller copiers).

When service calls come in from customers, they are received by a service clerk who identifies the machine in question and directs the request to the appropriate FSM. Since many customers have two or more different models of equipment, one call may be directed to two or more different FSMs, each of whom would send out a TSS to deal with the model they are responsible for. Although this may not sound efficient, it does not happen very often, and the Director of Technical Services strongly believes that by increasing the speed of repairs and reducing training costs, the gains from specialization outweigh any inefficiencies from specialization. In fact, the average number of machines serviced by a TSS has increased by about 20% since this policy was instituted, and the number of TSSs has been reduced accordingly.

Branch hours are from 8:30 a.m. to 5:00 p.m., and all TSSs are expected to adhere to these hours (so Duplox can avoid paying overtime), except in emergency situations that must be authorized by a field service manager. Since competition has been increasing in this tough market, and since company revenues and profitability levels have been slipping, expense budgets have been tightened in recent years, and the TSSs have been put under tighter control.

Minimum monthly, weekly, and daily productivity levels are strictly specified for each TSS, and there are strict quotas on repair expenses and travel expenses. Prior approval from an FSM is required for many actions even if they are within budget limitations. A TSS cannot order parts or tools needed for maintenance; all have to be ordered by the FSM, within strict dollar limits. Since there is often a delay in receiving the parts, in many cases the TSS that starts the job is not the TSS that finishes the job. Because of the large territory covered, quite a high level of TSS turnover, and the unpredictability of emergency calls, an individual TSS seldom visits the same customer twice in a row.

Chart 4

Duplox Copiers Canada Limited
Marketing Department

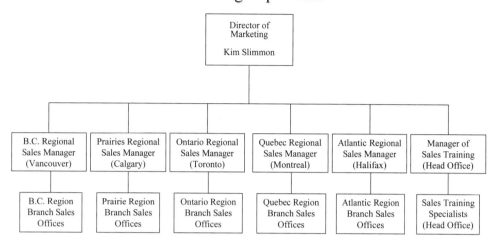

```
                    ┌─────────────────┐
                    │   Director of   │
                    │   Marketing     │
                    │                 │
                    │   Kim Slimmon   │
                    └─────────────────┘
```

B.C. Regional Sales Manager (Vancouver)	Prairies Regional Sales Manager (Calgary)	Ontario Regional Sales Manager (Toronto)	Quebec Regional Sales Manager (Montreal)	Atlantic Regional Sales Manager (Halifax)	Manager of Sales Training (Head Office)
B.C. Region Branch Sales Offices	Prairie Region Branch Sales Offices	Ontario Region Branch Sales Offices	Quebec Region Branch Sales Offices	Atlantic Region Branch Sales Offices	Sales Training Specialists (Head Office)

Chart 5

Marketing Department
Edmonton Branch
Sales Section

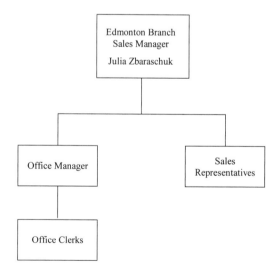

```
              ┌──────────────────────┐
              │  Edmonton Branch     │
              │  Sales Manager       │
              │                      │
              │  Julia Zbaraschuk    │
              └──────────────────────┘
```

Office Manager	Sales Representatives
Office Clerks	

When a TSS needs technical advice from head office, where there are numerous technical support experts who specialize in various types of machines, they are required to call their FSM, who first attempts to solve the problem himself, before calling the technical support department. (Chart 6 shows the structure of the Technical Training and Support Department.) One reason for the reluctance of the FSM to allow calls for technical support is that such calls are charged to the machine repair costs, something on which field service managers are evaluated.

There is generally little TSS discretion over maintenance schedules and services; they are to be performed strictly according to schedule. However, in one area TSSs are not required to "go by the book." In theory, all installations of new equipment have to meet company standards, in terms of space, ventilation, and wiring. But in practice, TSSs are not allowed to refuse installations that do not meet company specifications, unless they would result in safety problems.

This is because the director of marketing, regional and branch sales managers, and sales reps are mainly compensated based on volume of new installations, along with the volume of service contracts sold. (About 50% of the sales rep's direct pay is based on volume of sales and the remainder is base salary.) Sales reps are reluctant to tell customers that they should make expensive alterations to their facilities in order to install the machine, because they might lose the sale in this heavily competitive business. The executive committee has tacitly supported this practice, since they are evaluated by the parent firm on a combination of how many machines they sell as well as the profitability level of the Canadian operation.

Sales managers don't seem to put much weight on the argument by the TSSs that improper installation can cause higher repair and service costs. This frustrates many TSSs, especially since they are frequently criticized by sales staff for performing "shoddy service, which causes more breakdowns, and makes us look bad in the eyes of the customer."

TSSs are paid a flat monthly salary, plus overtime. Their performance is appraised once a year by the FSM, mainly based on how well they have adhered to productivity and expense standards, and merit raises are doled out by each FSM to one or two "deserving" TSSs each year. The director of technical services, the regional and branch service managers, and the FSMs are all paid on a salary-plus-bonus system. The bonus depends on whether TSS productivity met or exceeded standards in the past year, and whether repair and service expenses were below standard. These bonuses, if achieved, can double their earnings.

Compensation for the Director of Inventory Management and her two managers is based partly on minimizing inventory carrying charges. (Chart 7 shows the structure of the Inventory Management Department.) Compensation for the Director of Technical Training & Support is partly based on the level of cost recovery she can obtain from the Technical Services Department, and partly on keeping the overall cost of her Department.

Chart 6

Duplox Copiers Canada Limited
Technical Training and Support Department

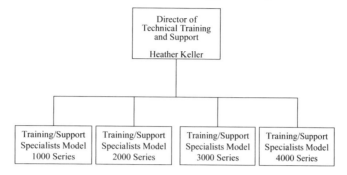

Chart 7

Duplox Copiers Canada Limited
Inventory Management Department

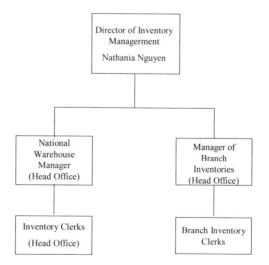

The Manager of Sales Training thinks that part of the sales problem is a lack of sufficient sales training for new sales reps. Compensation for the manager of sales training is based partly on the extent of recovery of training costs, as branch sales managers are required to charge sales training costs against their sales revenues, and "transfer" these amounts to the sales training function. The higher the transfers, the higher the bonus for the manager of sales training, but the lower the bonus for the branch sales manager.

Although employee benefits used to be good at Duplox, they have been whittled away in recent years in an attempt to cut costs as competition continues to intensify. (DCCL has a fixed benefits plan.) Right now, benefits are running at about 15% of total compensation, compared to the industry average of about 20%. Because turnover of TSSs has become a problem, total cash (direct) compensation for them remains above the industry averages. However, total cash compensation for the sales reps has dropped as sales (and therefore sales commissions) have dropped, and turnover among sales reps is becoming a serious problem.

Performance Results

Last year (2009), total revenues were $175,000,000, based on $90,000,000 of copier sales, $82,000,000 of service contracts, and $3,000,000 of warranty revenue. This produced a razor-thin profit of $4,000,000. The decline in profitability from the previous year would have been worse, but for the cuts in compensation costs resulting from a reduced number of TSSs (due to less sales and higher TSS productivity). The table below shows Duplox Canada's revenues, expenses, and profits for the past two years.

Revenues:	2008	2009
• Copier Sales:	$100,000,000	$ 90,000,000
• Service Contract Revenues:	$ 90,000,000	$ 82,000,000
• Warranty Revenue (received from Duplox Inc.):	$ 2,500,000	$ 3,000,000
Total Revenues:	*$192,500,000*	*$175,000,000*
Expenses:		
• Cost of copiers (67% of copier revenues)	$ 67,000,000	$ 60,300,000
• Cost of parts and supplies for service contracts: (25% of service revenues)	$ 22,500,000	$ 20,500,000
• Cost of parts and supplies for warranty work: (33% of warranty revenues)	$ 825,000	$ 1,000,000
• Total compensation costs	$ 82,000,000	$ 74,520,600
• Other costs (office costs, travel costs, etc.):	$ 15,000,000	$ 14,679,400
Total Expenses:	*$187,175,000*	*$171,000,000*
Profit:	*$ 5,175,000*	*$ 4,000,000*

Partial Listing of Duplox Job Descriptions

The following is a listing of some of the job descriptions currently used at Duplox Canada. While this list includes some of the most important jobs at Duplox, this list does not comprise all the different job descriptions used at Duplox. When designing and applying your job evaluation and pay-for-knowledge systems, this is the set of jobs you will apply them to.

Accountant (Finance and Administration Department)
Advertising & Product Promotion Specialist (Marketing Department)
Branch Inventory Clerk (Inventory Management Department)
Branch Sales Manager (Marketing Department)
Branch Service Manager (Technical Services Department)
Caretaker (Finance and Administration Department)
Compensation Clerk (Human Resources Department)
Compensation Manager (Human Resources Department)
Compensation Officer (Human Resources Department)
Director of Human Resources (Human Resources Department)
Director of Marketing (Marketing Department)
Director of Technical Services (Technical Services Department)
Director of Technical Training & Support Services (Technical Training & Support Department)
Field Service Manager (Technical Services Department)
Inventory Clerk (Inventory Management Department)
Manager of Branch Inventories (Inventory Management Department)
Regional Sales Manager (Marketing Department)
Sales Representative (Marketing Department)
Sales Training Specialist (Marketing Department)
Secretary (all departments)
Technical Service Specialist I – Model 1000 Series (Technical Services Department)
Technical Service Specialist I – Model 2000 Series (Technical Services Department)
Technical Service Specialist I – Model 3000 Series (Technical Services Department)
Technical Service Specialist I – Model 4000 Series (Technical Services Department)
Technical Service Specialist II – Model 1000 Series (Technical Services Department)
Technical Service Specialist II – Model 2000 Series (Technical Services Department)
Technical Service Specialist II – Model 3000 Series (Technical Services Department)
Technical Service Specialist II – Model 4000 Series (Technical Services Department)
Technical Service Specialist III – Model 1000 Series (Technical Services Department)
Technical Service Specialist III – Model 2000 Series (Technical Services Department)
Technical Service Specialist III – Model 3000 Series (Technical Services Department)
Technical Service Specialist III – Model 4000 Series (Technical Services Department)
Training/Support Specialist (Technical Training & Support Department)

Job Title: *ACCOUNTANT*
Department: Finance and Administration

Duties. Reporting to the Accounting Services Manager, accountants are required to perform administrative and support functions relating to operating accounts and capital equipment accounts. Accountants assist in preparation of monthly financial reporting, assist with year-end financial reporting and the year-end working paper file preparation, assist with review and implementation of financial and management accounting systems, and perform other accounting duties or projects that may be identified.

Desirable Qualifications. A commerce or business administration university degree, accompanied by a professional accounting designation, the ability to deal with moderately complex accounting issues; the ability to work with computer systems and electronic spreadsheets; the ability to relate well with other individuals; and good organizational, analytical, and communication skills.

Job Title: *ADVERTISING & PRODUCT PROMOTION SPECIALIST*
Department: Marketing

Duties. Under the supervision of the Director of Marketing, develops and recommends advertising and promotion policies that will assist the sales force in achieving profitable sales of equipment and services. Liaises with advertising and product promotion staff from parent company to ensure that sales campaigns and promotions are consistent with the desired company image and branding.

Desirable Qualifications. A university degree in commerce or business administration, specializing in advertising. At least two years experience as a sales representative for company products and services. Excellent verbal and written skills, and demonstrated creativity in sales approaches.

Job Title: *BRANCH INVENTORY CLERK*
Department: Inventory Management

Duties. Under the direction of Manager of Branch Inventories and the supervision of the Branch Service Manager, manages the parts inventory at the branch. Responsible for the security, proper storage, and proper disbursement of parts, and managing inventory levels to avoid shortages of parts authorized at the branch level or excess supply. Verifies and advises service specialists on appropriate part selection. Assists in acquiring appropriate parts from national warehouse.

Desirable Qualifications. Completion of grade 12, plus a one-year program in materials management at an appropriate technical institute. Good mathematical skills, and good communications ability, both verbal and written. Ability to comprehend technical documentation and parts manuals. Ability to work independently with little supervision.

Job Title: *BRANCH SALES MANAGER*
Department: Marketing

Duties. Under the general direction of the Regional Sales Manager, manages the marketing and sales of equipment and technical services that meet customer needs and will make a positive contribution to Duplox's financial performance in his/her branch. Ensures that contracted products will meet customer needs. May get involved in client negotiations over pricing issues. Prepares branch budgets and sales forecasts. Ensures that budgeted sales levels are accomplished. Evaluates current policies, procedures, and practices for achieving regional objectives, and implements improved policies, procedures, and practices. Responsible for selection, evaluation, coaching, promotion, transfer, or discharge of branch sales representatives. Supervises branch office manager and office clerks, and, in conjunction with the Branch Service Manager, oversees the administration of the branch.

Desirable Qualifications. This position requires a university commerce or business administration degree, with specialization in marketing. At least two years of experience in marketing/sales of company products and services. Demonstrated ability to coordinate, develop, and supervise staff, deal with interpersonal conflict, and meet departmental deadlines and performance objectives are essential. Excellent verbal and written communications skills.

Job Title: *BRANCH SERVICE MANAGER*
Department: Technical Services

Duties. Under the general supervision of the Regional Service Manager, manages the installation and servicing of company products at that branch. Supervises field service managers, and ensures that budgeted service revenue and cost targets are achieved for the branch. Evaluates current policies, procedures, and practices for achieving regional objectives, and implements improved policies, procedures, and practices. Responsible for selection, training, evaluation, coaching, promotion, transfer, or discharge of field service managers, technical service specialists, and service clerks. Supervises service clerks, and, in conjunction with the Manager of Branch Inventories, the Branch Inventory Clerk. In conjunction with the Branch Sales Manager, oversees the administration of the branch.

Desirable Qualifications. Applicant should have a two-year applied electronics designation from an accredited technical institute, and at least three years of experience as a Field Service Manager, preferably in the servicing of all models of company products. Demonstrated ability to coordinate, develop, and supervise staff, deal with interpersonal conflict, and meet departmental deadlines and performance objectives are essential. Excellent verbal and written communications skills.

Job Title: *CARETAKER*
Department: Finance and Administration (Facilities Management Section)

Duties. This person performs cleaning tasks both manually and using industrial-type scrubbing machines, under the general supervision of facilities managers. Duties include cleaning floors of halls, offices, and lavatories, using dry mop, wet mop, and broom. Operating industrial cleaning equipment in stripping, scrubbing, waxing, and polishing floors. Performing such minor repairs as replacing light bulbs, tightening or replacing screws in furniture, and maintaining cleaning equipment. Emptying and cleaning wastepaper baskets. Washing hand basins, toilet bowls, soap dishes, and other washroom equipment, and replenishing supplies of soap, towels, and toilet tissue. Opening and locking buildings at specified times. Moving furniture. Periodically washing walls, ceilings, windows, and doors. Reporting unusual circumstances such as vandalism, theft, and unauthorized persons. Providing all caretaking services as outlined in the *Caretaker Handbook*. Promoting good working relations with staff and customers. Performing related duties as assigned.

Desirable Qualifications. Elementary school education sufficient to provide skill in reading instructions. Good physical condition. Preferably experience in using hand- and power-operated cleaning equipment and cleaning materials.

Job Title: *COMPENSATION CLERK*
Department: Human Resources

Duties. Under the direction of the Compensation Officer, this person performs a variety of moderately complex clerical tasks associated with the compensation function. Although their work is supervised by the Compensation Manager, they are responsible for carrying out a series of clerical assignments without detailed instruction or review. These employees maintain cooperative and helpful relations in their contacts with other staff. Duties include: Setting up files for new employees. Coding and processing Payroll Authorization Forms, ensuring that appropriate deductions for benefits, tax, dues, and other factors are made. Overseeing preparation of paycheques or direct deposit of compensation. Creating records of employment for employees who are terminating. Making monthly remittance to the Receiver General, insurance programs, and other bodies. Answering enquiries of the Employment Insurance Commission concerning terminated employees or those on extended leave. Answering questions from employees about their paycheques and referring questions to other departments when appropriate.

Desirable Qualifications. Completion of Grade 12, preferably including or supplemented by courses in bookkeeping and introductory computing, including spreadsheets. Ability to enter data into computer systems accurately. Several years of clerical experience, preferably some of which in a compensation role.

Job Title: *COMPENSATION MANAGER*
Department: Human Resources

Duties. Under the direction of the Director of Human Resources, this position is responsible for managing the operation of the compensation system, including staffing, performance review, training and development of staff, and the hardware and software of a computer-based compensation administration system, as well as preparing and revising job descriptions and performing job evaluations. Will be responsible for implementing new compensation policies and monitoring their effectiveness on an ongoing basis, making necessary adjustments, and making recommendations for change. Will assist the Director of Human Resources in evaluating the effectiveness of existing compensation policies and formulating recommendations for changes to compensation policies.

Desirable Qualifications. A university degree in Commerce or Business administration with compensation and human resources course work, along with a CHRP (Certified Human Resources

Professional) designation. A minimum of five years of experience in compensation administration. Experience that demonstrates the following skills: ability to ability to relate well with other individuals and perform effective supervision; and excellent organization, analytical, and communication skills. Experience in the computer software industry would be an asset.

Job Title: *COMPENSATION OFFICER*
Department: Human Resources

Duties. Under the direction of the Compensation Manager, this position will be responsible for managing the day-to-day activities relating to the operation of the compensation system and for providing accounting support relating to the processing of base pay, performance pay, and benefits for employees. Will supervise several Compensation Clerks. Will stand in for the Compensation Manager when manager is absent.

Desirable Qualifications. A university degree in Commerce or Business Administration with course work in compensation systems and human resources, a CHRP (Certified Human Resources Professional) designation, and experience that will demonstrate the following skills: ability to deal with moderately complex accounting issues; ability to work with large computer systems in a complex environment; ability to work with electronic spreadsheets; ability to relate well with other individuals and perform effective supervision; and good organization, analytical, and communication skills.

Job Title: *DIRECTOR OF HUMAN RESOURCES*
Department: Human Resources

Duties. Under the general direction of the Vice President of Marketing and Administration, ensures the acquisition, training, retention, and motivation of personnel needed by Duplox to achieve its corporate goals. Evaluates human resource management strategy and organization design, and recommends new human resource policies to the executive committee when appropriate. Prepares departmental budget. Responsible for the selection, evaluation, and coaching of subordinate Human Resources managers. Evaluates current policies, procedures, and practices for achieving departmental objectives, and implements improved policies, procedures, and practices. Ensures that company compensation expenditures are deployed effectively. Recommends the most effective compensation and reward strategy and oversees the implementation of approved policies and strategies. Assists other departments in dealing effectively with human resources issues and problems. Provides support to top management in identifying strategic issues and trends affecting the company.

Desirable Qualifications. This position requires a university Commerce or Business Administration degree, with specialization in human resources, as well as additional course work at the post-graduate level, such as a Master of Business Administration with a specialization in human resources, and a CHRP (Certified Human Resources Professional) designation. At least ten years experience in human resource positions, with at least five years in the business equipment industry, and at least five years in a management capacity. Demonstrated ability to coordinate, develop, and supervise staff, deal with individual and group conflict, and meet departmental performance objectives are essential. Excellent verbal and written communications skills. Strong abilities to identify organizational problems and deal with them. Ability to cooperate effectively with and assist managers at a similar organizational level.

Job Title: *DIRECTOR OF MARKETING*
Department: Marketing

Duties. Under the general direction of the Vice President of Marketing and Administration, manages the marketing and sales of equipment and technical services that meet customer needs and will make a positive contribution to Duplox's financial performance. In conjunction with senior management, establishes the appropriate price guidelines for company products and services. Evaluates current marketing strategy and recommends new strategy to the executive committee when appropriate. Prepares sales forecasts for each fiscal year. Prepares departmental budget. Evaluates current policies, procedures, and practices for achieving departmental objectives, and implements improved policies, procedures, and practices. In conjunction with the Human Resources Department, responsible for selection, evaluation, and coaching of regional managers, and for ensuring that all sales staff receive proper training. Liaises with other Department Managers to ensure that overall corporate objectives are being accomplished. Provides support to top management in identifying strategic issues and trends affecting the company.

Desirable Qualifications. This position requires a university Commerce or Business Administration degree, with specialization in marketing, as well as additional marketing course work at the post-graduate level, such as a Master of Business Administration with a specialization in marketing. At least ten years of experience in marketing/sales of copiers, with at least five years in a management capacity. Demonstrated ability to coordinate, develop, and supervise staff, deal with individual and group conflict, and meet departmental deadlines and performance objectives are essential. Excellent verbal and written communications skills. Strong abilities to identify organizational problems and deal with them. Ability to cooperate effectively with managers at a similar organizational level.

Job Title: *DIRECTOR OF TECHNICAL SERVICES*
Department: Technical Services

Duties. Under the general direction of the Vice President of Field Services, manages the installation and servicing of copier equipment to satisfy contractual and warranty requirements, and to achieve budgeted revenue targets. Prepares departmental budget. Evaluates current policies, procedures, and practices for achieving departmental objectives, and implements improved policies, procedures, and practices. In conjunction with the Human Resources Department, responsible for selection, evaluation, and coaching of regional service managers. Liases with other Department Managers to ensure that overall corporate objectives are being accomplished. Provides support to top management in identifying strategic issues and trends affecting the company.

Desirable Qualifications. This position requires a university bachelors degree in engineering with a specialization in electronics products, as well as a commerce or business administration degree or Master of Business Administration degree, and at least ten years experience in managing servicing of copiers and/or allied business equipment. Demonstrated ability to coordinate, develop, and supervise staff, deal with individual and group conflict, and meet departmental deadlines and performance objectives are essential. Excellent verbal and written communications skills. Strong abilities to identify organizational problems and deal with them. Ability to cooperate effectively with managers at a similar organizational level.

Job Title: *DIRECTOR OF TECHNICAL TRAINING AND SUPPORT SERVICES*
Department: Technical Training & Support Services

Duties. Under the general direction of the Vice President of Field Services, manages the technical training and support of technical service specialists. Designs appropriate training programs for technical service specialists, and ensures that technical support is available to deal with any type of installation or servicing problem that may arise. Prepares departmental budget. Evaluates current policies, procedures, and practices for achieving departmental objectives, and implements improved policies, procedures, and practices. In conjunction with the Human Resources Department, responsible for selection, training, and evaluation of technical training/support specialists. Liases with other Department Managers to ensure that overall corporate objectives are being accomplished. Provides support to top management in identifying strategic issues and trends affecting the company.

Desirable Qualifications. This position requires a university bachelors and masters degree in engineering with a specialization in electronics products, and at least five years experience as a training/support specialist dealing with all types of company equipment, and course work in training theory and practice. Excellent verbal and written communications skills. Ability to cooperate effectively with managers at a similar organizational level.

Job Title: *FIELD SERVICE MANAGER*
Department: Technical Services

Duties. Under the supervision of the Branch Service Manager, manages the installation and servicing of company products for one of Model 1000, 2000, 3000, or 4000 series at that branch. Supervises technical service specialists for that model series, and ensures that all work is performed to company standards. Coordinates all task assignments for service to the model series under his/her purview, and scheduling of Technical Service Specialists. In conjunction with Branch Service Manager, sets minimum monthly, weekly, and daily productivity quotas for Technical Service Specialists, as well as repair and travel expenses, and ensures they are met. Orders all parts or tools needed for repairs. Ensures that appropriate training is given to all TSSs under their supervision. Advises Branch Service manager on the selection, evaluation, promotion, transfer, or discharge of technical service specialists.

Desirable Qualifications. Applicant should have a two-year applied electronics designation from an accredited technical institute, and at least three years of experience as a TSS III for that model series. Demonstrated ability to coordinate, develop, and supervise staff, deal with interpersonal conflict, and meet departmental deadlines and performance objectives are essential. Excellent verbal and written communications skills.

Job Title: *INVENTORY CLERK*
Department: Inventory Management (National Warehouse)

Duties. Under the direction of the National Warehouse Manager, responsible for the proper storage and proper disbursement of parts. Assists in managing inventory levels to avoid shortages of parts.

Desirable Qualifications. Completion of grade 12. Good clerical skills and good communications ability, both verbal and written. Ability to operate and comprehend computerized parts manuals.

Job Title: *MANAGER OF BRANCH INVENTORIES*
Department: Inventory Management

Duties: Under the supervision of the Director of Inventory Management, responsible for managing parts inventories at the branch offices. Uses computer models to ascertain whether particular parts should be maintained at the branch level, or in the national warehouse, and the most appropriate quantities of each part. Provides general direction for Branch Inventory Clerks, in conjunction with Branch Service Managers, who provide direct supervision. Advises Branch Managers on the selection of Branch Inventory Clerks, and is responsible for ensuring that they are following company policies.

Desirable Qualifications. A university degree in commerce or business administration, specializing in operations research and materials management. Effective communications skills, both verbal and written, and the ability to comprehend complex technical documentation.

Job Title: *REGIONAL SALES MANAGER*
Department: Marketing

Duties. Under the general direction of the Director of Marketing, manages the marketing and sales of equipment and technical services that meet customer needs and will make a positive contribution to Duplox's financial performance in his/her region. Prepares regional sales forecasts. Ensures that contracted products will meet customer needs. Within pricing guidelines established by senior management, sets prices for products and services that will contribute a satisfactory profit margin to Duplox. May get involved in client negotiations over pricing issues. Prepares regional budget. Ensures that budgeted sales levels are accomplished. Evaluates current policies, procedures, and practices for achieving regional objectives, and implements improved policies, procedures, and practices. Responsible for selection, evaluation, coaching, promotion, transfer, or discharge of branch sales managers. Jointly with Regional Service Manager, oversees administration of the regional office.

Desirable Qualifications. This position requires a university commerce or business administration degree, with specialization in marketing. At least three to five years of experience in marketing/sales of company products and services. Demonstrated ability to coordinate, develop, and supervise staff, deal with interpersonal conflict, and meet departmental deadlines and performance objectives are essential. Excellent verbal and written communications skills.

Job Title: *SALES REPRESENTATIVE*
Department: Marketing

Duties. Under the direction of the Branch Sales Manager, this person will be responsible for analyzing client needs and recommending appropriate equipment and service solutions; establishing and maintaining good working relationships with customers; disseminating information to clients on products and services available from the company; and maintaining customer satisfaction.

Desirable Qualifications. A university degree in commerce or business administration with a marketing concentration. A high customer service orientation; demonstrated interpersonal skills, such as the ability to establish equitable working relationships with staff and clients under pressure; demonstrated oral and written communication skills such as the proven ability to determine clients' needs, communicate solutions, answer client support questions, and respond to client requests with minimal supervision. Assets include a demonstrated ability to work independently and in a team as well as experience working in the business equipment field.

Job Title: *SALES TRAINING SPECIALIST*
Department: Marketing

Duties: Under the direction of the Manager of Sales Training, and in conjunction with the Department of Technical Training and Support Services, develops and conducts training programs for Sales Representatives. Programs include both technical knowledge and sales training.

Desirable Qualifications: A university degree in commerce or business administration, specializing in marketing and training. At least two years of experience as a Sales Representative. Excellent verbal and written communications skills and interpersonal skills. Demonstrated ability to organize and make effective presentations.

Job Title: *SECRETARY*
Departments: All

Duties. These individuals provide secretarial and administrative support to Directors and Managers, and perform responsible, varied, and complex clerical tasks. The assignments typically require the use of a broad understanding of the structure and division of responsibility, and functions of the units they service. Expected to take initiative in relieving Directors/Managers of administrative detail that does not require the application of professional judgement. This may involve drafting letters and maintaining records on budget allotments, expenditures, commitments, and residual balances. Screening of phone and office calls, setting up appointments, answering questions, and referring visitors to appropriate individuals.

Desirable Qualifications. Grade 12 plus completion of secretarial/administrative assistant training program, with working knowledge of word processing, spreadsheet, and related programs. Excellent verbal and written communication skills. A minimum of two years of workplace experience.

Job Title: *TECHNICAL SERVICE SPECIALIST I – MODEL 1000 SERIES*
Department: Technical Services

Duties. Under the general supervision of the Field Service Manager, performs routine product installations and routine product servicing for all products within the Model 1000 series. Assists TSS II or III in complex product installations, product breakdowns, and major product overhauls.

Desirable Qualifications. Applicant should have a two-year applied electronics designation from an accredited technical institute. The successful applicant must be able to respond constructively to feedback and direction, and to develop and learn new skills as required.

Job Title: *TECHNICAL SERVICE SPECIALIST I – MODEL 2000 SERIES*
Department: Technical Services

Duties. Under the general supervision of the Field Service Manager, performs routine product installations and routine product servicing for all products within the Model 2000 series. Assists TSS II or III in complex product installations, product breakdowns, and major product overhauls.

Desirable Qualifications. Applicant should have a two-year applied electronics designation from an accredited technical institute. The successful applicant must be able to respond constructively to feedback and direction, and to develop and learn new skills as required.

Job Title: *TECHNICAL SERVICE SPECIALIST I – MODEL 3000 SERIES*
Department: Technical Services

Duties. Under the general supervision of the Field Service Manager, performs routine product installations and routine product servicing for all products within the Model 3000 series. Assists TSS II or III in complex product installations, product breakdowns, and major product overhauls.

Desirable Qualifications. Applicant should have a two-year applied electronics designation from an accredited technical institute. The successful applicant must be able to respond constructively to feedback and direction, and to develop and learn new skills as required.

Job Title: *TECHNICAL SERVICE SPECIALIST I – MODEL 4000 SERIES*
Department: Technical Services

Duties. Under the general supervision of the Field Service Manager, performs routine product installations and routine product servicing for all products within the Model 4000 series. Assists TSS II or III in complex product installations, product breakdowns, and major product overhauls.

Desirable Qualifications. Applicant should have a two-year applied electronics designation from an accredited technical institute. The successful applicant must be able to respond constructively to feedback and direction, and to develop and learn new skills as required.

Job Title: *TECHNICAL SERVICE SPECIALIST II – MODEL 1000 SERIES*
Department: Technical Services

Duties. Under the general supervision of the Field Service Manager, performs complex product installations, repair of product breakdowns and malfunctions, and adjustment of quality problems for all products in the Model 1000 series. Supervises and trains TSS I in these functions, and performs the initial on-the-job training for TSS I as required. Assists TSS III in major malfunctions, and with major product overhauls.

Desirable Qualifications. Applicant should have a two-year applied electronics designation from an accredited technical institute, and at least one year of experience in servicing of Model 1000 products. The successful applicant must be able to work independently with little or no supervision, to respond constructively to feedback and direction, to develop and learn new skills as required, and to effectively instruct TSS I in their job duties and prepare them for more complex duties. Effective customer relations skills are essential.

Job Title: *TECHNICAL SERVICE SPECIALIST II – MODEL 2000 SERIES*
Department: Technical Services

Duties. Under the general supervision of the Field Service Manager, performs complex product installations, repair of product breakdowns and malfunctions, and adjustment of quality problems for all products in the Model 2000 series. Supervises and trains TSS I in these functions, and performs the initial on-the-job training for TSS I as required. Assists TSS III in major malfunctions, and with major product overhauls.

Desirable Qualifications. Applicant should have a two-year applied electronics designation from an accredited technical institute, and at least one year of experience in servicing of Model 2000 products. The successful applicant must be able to work independently with little or no supervision, to respond constructively to feedback and direction, to develop and learn new skills as required, and to effectively instruct TSS I in their job duties and prepare them for more complex duties. Effective customer relations skills are essential.

Job Title: *TECHNICAL SERVICE SPECIALIST II – MODEL 3000 SERIES*
Department: Technical Services

Duties. Under the general supervision of the Field Service Manager, performs complex product installations, repair of product breakdowns and malfunctions, and adjustment of quality problems for all products in the Model 3000 series. Supervises and trains TSS I in these functions, and performs the initial on-the-job training for TSS I as required. Assists TSS III in major malfunctions, and with major product overhauls.

Desirable Qualifications. Applicant should have a two-year applied electronics designation from an accredited technical institute, and at least one year of experience in servicing of Model 3000 products. The successful applicant must be able to work independently with little or no supervision, to respond constructively to feedback and direction, to develop and learn new skills as required, and to effectively instruct TSS I in their job duties and prepare them for more complex duties. Effective customer relations skills are essential.

Job Title: *TECHNICAL SERVICE SPECIALIST II – MODEL 4000 SERIES*
Department: Technical Services

Duties. Under the general supervision of the Field Service Manager, performs complex product installations, repair of product breakdowns and malfunctions, and adjustment of quality problems for all products in the Model 4000 series. Supervises and trains TSS I in these functions, and performs the initial on-the-job training for TSS I as required. Assists TSS III in major malfunctions, and with major product overhauls.

Desirable Qualifications. Applicant should have a two-year applied electronics designation from an accredited technical institute, and at least one year of experience in servicing of Model 4000 products. The successful applicant must be able to work independently with little or no supervision, to respond constructively to feedback and direction, to develop and learn new skills as required, and to effectively instruct TSS I in their job duties and prepare them for more complex duties. Effective customer relations skills are essential.

Job Title: *TECHNICAL SERVICE SPECIALIST III – MODEL 1000 SERIES*
Department: Technical Services

Duties. Under the general supervision of the Field Service Manager, performs complex product installations, repair of major product breakdowns and malfunctions, adjustment of complex quality problems, and complex overhauls for all products in the Model 1000 series. Supervises and trains TSS II in these functions. In cooperation with the Field Services Manager, may assist Sales Representatives in identification of the technical configuration of equipment that best suits customer needs.

Desirable Qualifications. Applicant should have a two-year applied electronics designation from an accredited technical institute, and at least two years of experience at the TSS II level in the servicing of Model 1000 products. The successful applicant must be able to work independently with little or no supervision, to respond constructively to feedback and direction, to develop and learn new skills as required, to effectively instruct TSS II in their job duties, and to prepare them for more complex duties. Ability to comprehend complex technical documentation is essential. Successful completion of all factory-approved technical training modules for Model 1000 series equipment.

Job Title: *TECHNICAL SERVICE SPECIALIST III – MODEL 2000 SERIES*
Department: Technical Services

Duties. Under the general supervision of the Field Service Manager, performs complex product installations, repair of major product breakdowns and malfunctions, adjustment of complex quality problems, and complex overhauls for all products in the Model 2000 series. Supervises and trains TSS II in these functions. In cooperation with the Field Services Manager, may assist Sales Representatives in identification of the technical configuration of equipment that best suits customer needs.

Desirable Qualifications. Applicant should have a two-year applied electronics designation from an accredited technical institute, and at least two years of experience at the TSS II level in the servicing of Model 2000 products. The successful applicant must be able to work independently with little or no supervision, to respond constructively to feedback and direction, to develop and learn new skills as required, to effectively instruct TSS II in their job duties, and to prepare them for more complex duties. Ability to comprehend complex technical documentation is essential. Successful completion of all factory-approved technical training modules for Model 2000 series equipment.

Job Title: *TECHNICAL SERVICE SPECIALIST III – MODEL 3000 SERIES*
Department: Technical Services

Duties. Under the general supervision of the Field Service Manager, performs complex product installations, repair of major product breakdowns and malfunctions, adjustment of complex quality problems, and complex overhauls for all products in the Model 3000 series. Supervises and trains TSS II in these functions. In cooperation with the Field Services Manager, may assist Sales Representatives in identification of the technical configuration of equipment that best suits customer needs.

Desirable Qualifications. Applicant should have a two-year applied electronics designation from an accredited technical institute, and at least two years of experience at the TSS II level in the servicing of Model 3000 products. The successful applicant must be able to work independently with little or no supervision, to respond constructively to feedback and direction, to develop and learn new skills as required, to effectively instruct TSS II in their job duties, and to prepare them for more complex duties. Ability to comprehend complex technical documentation is essential. Successful completion of all factory-approved technical training modules for Model 3000 series equipment.

Job Title: *TECHNICAL SERVICE SPECIALIST III – MODEL 4000 SERIES*
Department: Technical Services

Duties. Under the general supervision of the Field Service Manager, performs complex product installations, repair of major product breakdowns and malfunctions, adjustment of complex quality problems, and complex overhauls for all products in the Model 4000 series. Supervises and trains TSS II in these functions. In cooperation with the Field Services Manager, may assist Sales Representatives in identification of the technical configuration of equipment that best suits customer needs.

Desirable Qualifications. Applicant should have a two-year applied electronics designation from an accredited technical institute, and at least two years of experience at the TSS II level in the servicing of Model 4000 products. The successful applicant must be able to work independently with little or no supervision, to respond constructively to feedback and direction, to develop and learn new skills as required, to effectively instruct TSS II in their job duties, and to prepare them for more complex duties. Ability to comprehend complex technical documentation is essential. Successful completion of all factory-approved technical training modules for Model 4000 series equipment.

Job Title: TRAINING/SUPPORT SPECIALIST
Department: Technical Training & Support

Duties: Under the direction of the Director of Technical Training & Support, develops and conducts technical training programs for Technical Support Specialists for a given Model series. Provides direct support to Field Service Managers via telephone or email to deal with complex problems for this model series. Assists Sales Training Specialists in the marketing department with preparation of training materials and programs for sales representatives.

Desirable Qualifications: A university degree in engineering, specializing in electronic products. At least two years of experience as a TSS III for that particular model series. Excellent verbal and written communications skills and interpersonal skills. Demonstrated ability to organize and make effective presentations.

Zenith Medical Systems Incorporated

Your Client Firm

Your client firm is Zenith Medical Services Incorporated. Zenith was formed in 2007 as a joint venture of a major computer firm and a leading supplier of hospital products. Both firms invested an equal amount of capital in the venture. Top management for Zenith was provided from the ranks of the parent companies, but the majority of top management, including the CEO of Zenith, came from the hospital products firm. The logic for this was that managers from the hospital products firm would have a greater grounding in the health care industry than would managers from the computer firm.

Zenith's product is information management systems for health care institutions. As health care organizations have become more complex, there has been an increasing demand for computer systems that will help manage the massive flows of information necessary for their effective operation. The idea is to develop an integrated system for patient records, staff and facilities scheduling, materials management, medication tracking, and financial management, in place of the separate systems that now exist in most cases. Ineffective transmission of information between different parties who need that information makes for an inefficient operation and could even cost lives. Zenith would be a comprehensive provider of these systems, handling everything from systems design to installation, training, and maintenance.

Zenith has about 600 employees, with about half located at head office in Ottawa and half located at five regional offices dispersed across Canada. Chart 1 shows the organization structure at head office. The executive committee consists of the CEO and the two vice presidents. There are six main departments. Marketing, Finance/Accounting, and Human Resources report to Jeff Wieler, Vice President Marketing and Administration, while Systems Development, Systems Installation, and Systems Maintenance report to Rob McIvor, Vice President Systems. Most of the marketing and systems maintenance employees are dispersed across the five regional offices, while the other departments are located at head office in Ottawa.

Although some employees were seconded from the parent companies, most were hired on the open market or from the companies that Zenith took over. Early in the firm's life, Zenith took over a number of small software companies that specialized in specific systems. For example, they took over a firm that specialized in medication tracking systems, another that specialized in systems for hospital scheduling, and another that produced systems for patient records.

Darlene Adams, President and CEO of Zenith Medical Systems, has requested your consulting services, and is delighted that your team was assigned to her firm. Zenith is experiencing serious performance problems: employee turnover is up and morale is down; customer satisfaction is down and complaints are up; and, most importantly, revenue and profits are both down. President Adams knows that the compensation system used by a firm can contribute to all these problems, and since compensation is a major cost item for her firm (currently accounting for about 79% of the firm's costs) she suspects that the firm's compensation system may be implicated in these problems. But she can't be sure without your help.

Chart 1

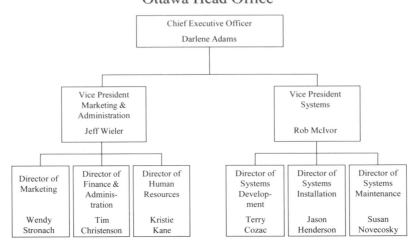

Zenith Medical Systems Incorporated
Organization Chart
Ottawa Head Office

Because President Adams recognizes that compensation is just one of several important structural variables that must all fit together if effective organizational performance is to occur, you are authorized to suggest any changes to the managerial strategy and structure of the organization needed to make the new compensation system work. Your only limitation is that she wants no changes to be made to the company's six-department structure, which she believes is the best way to organize. Beyond that, you have free rein to make recommendations about reward structure, job design, and the other structural elements.

Zenith Operations and Structure

Virtually all of the 600 employees at Zenith have university degrees, most of them in software design and computer programming, but also in the other functional areas, such as finance, marketing, and human resource management. Employees are well paid in order to attract outstanding individuals. Pay for most employees is based on a fixed monthly salary, with annual reviews, at which time it is normal to receive a pay raise. It is extremely unusual not to receive a pay raise at this time.

Because management knew that the firm was relatively new and had no common culture, and because people are the key component of a software firm (approximately 70% to 75% of all expenses are compensation expenses for most software firms), the company adopted a number of policies to encourage employee loyalty, such as increased vacation after two and then five years, and liberal employee benefits. Employee benefits amount to about 30% of total compensation costs (compared to an industry average of about 20%). Total compensation for the most recent fiscal year (2009) was $43,665,820.

The job of Marketing is to bring in the contracts for systems. The department is organized geographically, as Chart 2 shows, with regional offices in Vancouver, Edmonton, Toronto,

Montreal, and Halifax. Each systems marketing specialist is assigned a specific geographical area. Within that area, they are expected to contact all health care institutions and attempt to sell them systems. Sales personnel are paid a base salary plus commission based on a percentage of the total value of systems contracts that are signed in their territory. To motivate marketing specialists, base pay is set low, and the expectation is that at least half of a marketing rep's income should come from commissions.

Chart 2

Zenith Medical Systems Incorporated
Marketing Department

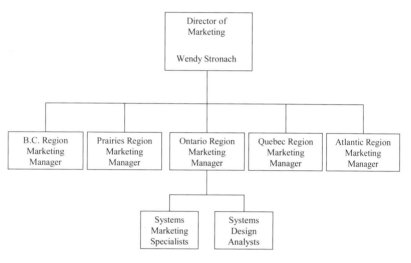

Note: All regional offices have a structure identical to the Ontario regional office.

Once an institution agrees to purchase a system, the marketing specialist and a systems design specialist in the marketing department work to establish the exact characteristics and parameters for the system, based on the stated needs of the client and the hardware they will be using. The cost of the system is then estimated, according to strict guidelines set by top management, a purchase price is established, and the delivery schedule is determined. Finally, a contract is signed, detailing all of this.

The procedures for doing all this are very strictly laid out, and marketing has very little discretion on the sales price. (Prices are fairly competitive, but not usually the lowest in the industry.) Since they have little flexibility on price, in order to close a deal the marketing rep often promised extra features and quick delivery. Managers in the marketing department are evaluated on the number of contracts signed and their dollar value. The marketing department manager is paid a modest base salary plus a substantial bonus, depending on the extent to which sales targets are met or exceeded, as are the regional marketing managers.

Once signed, the contract goes to the Systems Development Department (see Chart 3), which first attempts to see whether a previously designed system can be used as a basis for the new system. Each contract is broken down into segments, and one or more applications programmers are assigned to work on each segment. Procedures for so doing are carefully laid out. Systems integration specialists are given the task of ensuring that all parts of the system fit together.

Top management evaluates managers in the Systems Development Department in terms of whether systems are completed by the development date set when the contract was signed, and whether each system is within the budgeted development hours for the project. Managers in the systems development department are paid a base salary plus a large bonus if they meet or exceed these targets. Non-managerial employees in the Systems Development Department receive base pay plus indirect pay only, as do all non-managerial employees except systems marketing reps.

Once the Systems Development Department has a system that they believe meets contract specifications, it is passed on to the Systems Installations Department (see Chart 4). Their job is to take the system to the client, install it on client hardware, help with any necessary data conversion, test the system, and conduct training for client personnel. For each installation, a team of systems installation employees is sent out from head office, where they are based. Managers in the Systems Installations Department are evaluated on whether installations are completed by the date specified in the contract, and within total budgeted hours for each installation. Managers are paid a base salary plus a large bonus, dependent on meeting or exceeding these targets.

If problems arise after installation, or if changes to the system become necessary, due to changing information requirements or changing hardware (which are both frequent occurrences), the role of the Systems Maintenance Department (see Chart 5) is to deal with these problems. If the problem is the fault of Zenith, the work is done free of charge. If the work is additional work requested by the customer, the department charges a standard per hour fee. To be close to customers, the systems maintenance staff are located at the five regional offices, with a regional maintenance manager at each. Maintenance department managers are paid a base salary plus a bonus based on a percentage of the extra revenue the department generates.

In order to build market share as quickly as possible, the marketing department seeks to sell to any health care institution that will purchase a system, even if there is not much profit in it for Zenith. Their clients vary enormously. Some clients are large university teaching hospitals, with literally dozens of medical specialties. Some clients are very specialized, such as a cancer clinic, or a special care nursing home. No two clients are alike, in terms of their information needs, their current systems, or their current hardware. Every system sold requires at least some modification from the standard product, and most require very substantial modification.

The competitive environment is intense. The biggest firm in the industry (based in the United States, but also selling in Canada) does about half a billion dollars in sales annually, while Zenith was expected to do about 10% of that during its first two years. (Projected sales for the first year were targeted at $55,000,000, and $60,000,000 for the second year. Top management expected the firm to break even the first year, and show a $3,000,000 profit the second year.) Zenith is the largest medical systems firm based in Canada, and the eighth-largest medical systems company in North America. It would be considered a middle-sized firm in the industry.

Chart 3

Zenith Medical Systems Incorporated
Systems Development Department

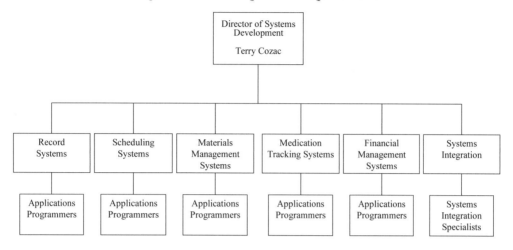

Chart 4

Zenith Medical Systems Incorporated
Systems Installations Department

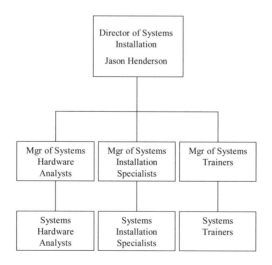

Chart 5

Zenith Medical Systems Incorporated
Systems Maintenance Department

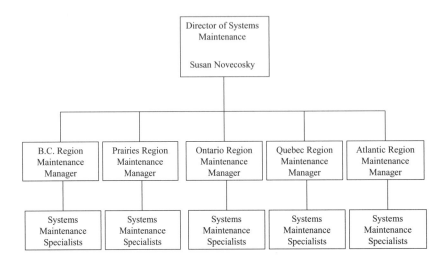

The competitive strategy for the biggest firms in the industry is to compete on price and speed of delivery. Because of their size, the biggest firms have an extensive "inventory" of standardized systems, from which the client was essentially expected to select one. Some modifications could be made, but clients are expected to basically accept the system provided and adapt to it. Because of their resulting low development costs, the big firms can pass these savings on to their clients. They are also able to provide fast delivery dates. To make sure their systems stay up to date as technology and the information needs of clients change, the large firms each had an applied research department constantly updating their basic systems. In this field, both the available hardware and the information needs of clients change quite rapidly, as new medical and technological innovations are discovered.

The small firms in the industry compete in one of three ways. Some firms specialize in one type of health care institution, such as nursing homes, or geriatric hospitals, and tend to have one basic specialized product. Others focus on one particular systems module, often doing subcontracting work for larger medical systems firms. Still others essentially work from scratch, designing customized systems for institutions that are not happy with the standardized systems that are available on the market.

Performance Results

Zenith's first year (2008) was quite promising, with a net loss of about $1,000,000 on sales of $58,000,000. Marketing had exceeded objectives, and Systems Development had met expectations, but Systems Installations was consistently late with final installation and over budget, and Systems Maintenance was way under revenue projections.

Top management was not overly concerned, since they expected these problems would iron out over time. They expected that increased revenues would bring economies of scale, which would increase profitability. But they did feel that something needed to be done about what they saw as the poor performance of the systems installations and maintenance departments, so they replaced the managers of these departments (who had both come from the parent computer firm) with executives from the parent hospital products firm.

To management's dismay, sales actually dropped the following year (2009), to $50,000,000, which produced a net loss of $5,000,000. Moreover, customers are unhappy because systems are late in being brought up and running, don't perform as promised by the sales force, are subject to frequent crashes, and because Systems Maintenance seems to show little enthusiasm for fixing these problems.

The morale of the sales force, which had been quite high at the outset, sank as sales (and their sales commissions) declined. Because of the poor reputation the company's products are beginning to get, marketing reps are finding that they have to promise more and more special features to get any contracts at all, and are desperately trying to close any deal they can get.

Morale is generally low throughout the company, with employees focusing only on their own jobs, feeling little need or desire to cooperate with workers in other departments. Indeed, most employees view other departments as populated mainly by obnoxious incompetents. For example, the Systems Installations Department frequently find that the systems provided by the Systems Development Department need extensive rework to get them operating at all, and this makes it very difficult or impossible to meet their installation guidelines. But when Installations complains to Systems Development, they themselves are accused of being incompetent.

Systems Development believes that any installation problems are due to either the incompetence of the personnel in the Installations Department, or the inability of the Marketing Department to accurately understand and convey customer requirements—most probably, both! By the end of the second year, Systems Development found it more and more difficult to meet their targets as the systems that were promised to customers grew fancier, but there was no increase in the price to customers, and no increase in the time and hours budgeted for each system. By the end of the second year, they found that they were not meeting client timelines for most systems, and were consistently over budgeted hours.

Because Installations often does not even receive the system until after the targeted date for completion of installation, installation timelines are almost never met, and clients usually unload their displeasure on Installations staff when they do arrive. In response, the new Installations Department manager ordered staff to "just get the basic system up and running as fast as possible; we'll worry about the fancy details later." Since targeted customer delivery dates were almost never met, he was determined to at least bring in as many projects as possible within budgeted hours. He believed that extensive systems testing was an unnecessary expense, and cut back on time devoted to this, as well as time spent on training client staff. With these measures, he was able to bring in some projects under budgeted hours.

Systems Maintenance are finding that they are spending virtually all their time dealing with frequent "crashes" of systems, and dealing with complaints that special features that the marketing rep had promised either don't work right or don't work at all. Sometimes features are missing entirely. As a result, the Maintenance Department is forced to spend most of its time repairing crashes or adding the promised features themselves. They are able to spend virtually no time on activities that will generate revenue. In response, they are trying to charge clients for systems failures that are caused by client staff, which are growing more frequent. But clients object strenuously to this policy, claiming that the crashes are actually Zenith's fault due to poorly designed systems or inadequate training of client staff.

Systems Maintenance blames Systems Development for creating poor systems, Systems Installations for faulty installation, and Marketing for providing the client with unrealistic expectations of what the system would be able to do. They are especially bitter because, although they haven't caused the problems, they are always the ones berated by panicky, frustrated, angry customers when they show up to repair a crashed system. Employee turnover in this department is the highest in the company, although it is becoming a serious problem everywhere.

Marketing views all three systems departments as incompetent, and believes that the poor quality of their work is making it almost impossible to sell company products. Overall, relations between all departments are very bitter, and personnel in each department try to avoid talking to anyone in the other departments unless absolutely necessary.

Top management is concerned about these problems. However, they believe that problems like these are to be expected in any new company, and will turn around, given sufficient time. Indeed, it is very normal for a new company to lose money in its first year or two as it attempts to enter a market and gain market share. Revenues often lag expenses, since it is necessary to establish some basic products in order to have something to sell. It often takes a while to get the bugs out of new products, and to get work structures operating effectively. Also, it takes time for a common corporate culture to emerge, to help bind the company together.

But while waiting for all this to happen, something had to be done in the meantime. To deal with the immediate problem of late product delivery and customer dissatisfaction with product quality, they replaced the Director of the Systems Development Department (a former computer company executive) with a manager from the hospital supplies parent. To deal with the problem of decreasing sales, they authorized the hiring of more systems marketing specialists. To ensure that correct decisions are being made, they reemphasized the existing policy that all important decisions are to come up through the hierarchy to top management for approval. Finally, to increase the firm's operating capital, the two parent companies are planning to list Zenith on the Toronto Stock Exchange within the next few months, with each parent company retaining 30% of the shares.

Partial Listing of Zenith Job Descriptions

The following is a listing of some of the job descriptions currently used at Zenith. While this list includes some of the most important jobs at Zenith, this list does not comprise all of the different job descriptions used at Zenith. When designing and applying your job evaluation and pay-for-knowledge systems, this is the set of jobs you will apply them to.

Accountant (Finance and Administration Department)
Junior Applications Programmer – Financial Management Systems
Junior Applications Programmer – Materials Management Systems
Junior Applications Programmer – Medication Tracking Systems
Junior Applications Programmer – Records Systems
Junior Applications Programmer – Scheduling Systems
Intermediate Applications Programmer – Financial Management Systems
Intermediate Applications Programmer – Materials Management Systems
Intermediate Applications Programmer – Medication Tracking Systems
Intermediate Applications Programmer – Records Systems
Intermediate Applications Programmer – Scheduling Systems
Senior Applications Programmer – Financial Management Systems
Senior Applications Programmer – Materials Management Systems
Senior Applications Programmer – Medication Tracking Systems
Senior Applications Programmer – Records Systems
Senior Applications Programmer – Scheduling Systems
Caretaker (Finance and Administration Department)
Compensation Clerk (Human Resources Department)
Compensation Officer (Human Resources Department)
Compensation Manager (Human Resources Department)
Director of Human Resources (Human Resources Department)
Director of Marketing (Marketing Department)
Director of Systems Development (Systems Development Department)
Manager of Financial Systems Development (Systems Development Department)
Regional Marketing Manager (Marketing Department)
Secretary (all departments)
Systems Design Analyst (Marketing Department)
Senior Systems Hardware Analyst (Installation Department)
Senior Systems Installation Specialist (Installation Department)
Systems Integration Specialist (Systems Development Department)
Systems Marketing Specialist (Marketing Department)
Junior Systems Trainer (Systems Installation Department)

Job Title: *ACCOUNTANT*
Department: Finance and Administration (Accounting Services Section)

Duties. Reporting to the Accounting Services Manager, accountants are required to perform administrative and support functions relating to operating accounts and capital equipment accounts. Accountants assist in preparation of monthly financial reporting, assist with year-end financial reporting and the year-end working paper file preparation, assist with review and implementation of financial and management accounting systems, and perform other accounting duties or projects which may be identified.

Desirable Qualifications. A commerce or business administration university degree, accompanied by a professional accounting designation; the ability to deal with moderately complex accounting issues; the ability to work with computer systems and electronic spreadsheets; the ability to relate well with other individuals; and good organizational, analytical, and communication skills.

Job Title: *JUNIOR APPLICATIONS PROGRAMMER – FINANCIAL MANAGEMENT SYSTEMS*
Department: Systems Development (Financial Management Systems Section)

Duties. Under the supervision of Intermediate or Senior Applications Programmers, applies knowledge of computer capabilities, subject matter, and symbolic logic to convert detailed logical flow chart to language processable by computer for the operation of billing, payment, and financial information systems. Enters program codes into computer system. Inputs test data into computer. Observes computer monitor to interpret program operating codes and to detect basic errors. On instructions from more senior staff, corrects program errors, using methods such as modifying program or altering sequence of program steps.

Desirable Qualifications. Applicant should have a university degree in Computer Science with a demonstrable knowledge of good programming practices, including software configuration management. The successful applicant must be able to respond constructively to feedback and direction. Assets would include: familiarity with one or more of the commonly used software products (especially relational database management systems such as Rdb or Oracle) as well as application generators such as RALLY or OracleForms, COBOL, or Datatrieve; and work experience in applications programming.

Job Title: *JUNIOR APPLICATIONS PROGRAMMER – MATERIALS MANAGEMENT SYSTEMS*
Department: Systems Development (Materials Management Systems Section)

Duties. Under the supervision of Intermediate or Senior Applications Programmers, applies knowledge of computer capabilities, subject matter, and symbolic logic to convert detailed logical flow chart to language processable by computer for the operation of integrated purchasing and inventory control systems. Enters program codes into computer system. Inputs test data into computer. Observes computer monitor to interpret program operating codes and to detect basic errors. On instructions from more senior staff, corrects program errors, using methods such as modifying program or altering sequence of program steps.

Desirable Qualifications. Applicant should have a university degree in computer science with a demonstrable knowledge of good programming practices, including software configuration management. The successful applicant must be able to respond constructively to feedback and direction. Assets would include: familiarity with one or more of the commonly used software products (especially a relational database management system such as Rdb or Oracle) and application generators such as RALLY or OracleForms, COBOL or Datatrieve; and work experience in applications programming.

Job Title: *JUNIOR APPLICATIONS PROGRAMMER – MEDICATION TRACKING SYSTEMS*
Department: Systems Development (Medication Tracking Systems Section)

Duties. Under the supervision of Intermediate or Senior Applications Programmers, applies knowledge of computer capabilities, subject matter, and symbolic logic to convert detailed logical flow chart to language processable by computer for the operation of medication tracking systems. Enters program codes into computer system. Inputs test data into computer. Observes computer monitor screen to interpret program operating codes and to detect basic errors. On instructions from more senior staff, corrects program errors, using methods such as modifying program or altering sequence of program steps.

Desirable Qualifications. Applicant should have a university degree in Computer Science with a demonstrable knowledge of good programming practices, including software configuration management. The successful applicant must be able to respond constructively to feedback and direction. Assets would include: familiarity with one or more of the commonly used software products (especially a relational database management system such as Rdb or Oracle) and application generators such as RALLY or OracleForms, COBOL or Datatrieve; and work experience in applications programming.

Job Title: *JUNIOR APPLICATIONS PROGRAMMER – RECORDS SYSTEMS*
Department: Systems Development (Record Systems Section)

Duties. Under the supervision of Intermediate or Senior Applications Programmers, applies knowledge of computer capabilities, subject matter, and symbolic logic to convert detailed logical flow chart to language processable by computer for the operation of patient and employee record keeping systems. Enters program codes into computer system. Inputs test data into computer. Observes computer monitor screen to interpret program operating codes and to detect basic errors. On instructions from more senior staff, corrects program errors, using methods such as modifying program or altering sequence of program steps.

Desirable Qualifications. Applicant should have a university degree in Computer Science with a demonstrable knowledge of good programming practices, including software configuration management. The successful applicant must be able to respond constructively to feedback and direction. Assets would include: familiarity with one or more of the commonly used software products (especially a relational database management system such as Rdb or Oracle) and application generators such as RALLY or OracleForms, COBOL or Datatrieve; and work experience in applications programming.

Job Title: *JUNIOR APPLICATIONS PROGRAMMER – SCHEDULING SYSTEMS*
Department: Systems Development (Scheduling Systems Section)

Duties. Under the supervision of Intermediate or Senior Applications Programmers, applies knowledge of computer capabilities, subject matter, and symbolic logic to convert detailed logical flow chart to language processable by computer for the operation of patient, staff, facilities scheduling systems. Enters program codes into computer system. Inputs test data into computer. Observes computer monitor to interpret program operating codes and to detect basic errors. On instructions from more senior staff, corrects program errors, using methods such as modifying program or altering sequence of program steps.

Desirable Qualifications. Applicant should have a university degree in Computer Science with a demonstrable knowledge of good programming practices, including software configuration management. The successful applicant must be able to respond constructively to feedback and direction. Assets would include familiarity with one or more of the commonly used software products (especially a relational database management system such as Rdb or Oracle) and application generators such as RALLY or OracleForms, COBOL or Datatrieve; and work experience in applications programming.

Job Title: *INTERMEDIATE APPLICATIONS PROGRAMMER – FINANCIAL MANAGEMENT SYSTEMS*
Department: Systems Development (Financial Management Systems Section)

Duties. Under the general supervision of a Senior Applications Programmer, converts data from project specifications and detailed workflow chart to create or modify computer integrated billing, payments, and financial information programs. Receives from Senior Applications Programmer detailed workflow chart and diagram that illustrates sequence of steps that program must follow and describes input, output, and logical operations involved. Analyzes workflow chart and diagram, applying knowledge of computer capabilities, subject matter, and symbolic logic. Converts detailed logical flow chart to language processable by computer. Supervises entry of program codes into computer system and inputting of test data. Observes computer monitor screen to interpret program operating codes. Corrects program errors, using methods such as modifying program or altering sequence of program steps. Writes program documentation and instructions to guide client personnel in system operations. May direct and coordinate work of Junior Applications Programmers to write, test, and modify computer programs.

Desirable Qualifications. Applicant should have a university degree in Computer Science with a minimum of one year of work experience in financial management software, and a demonstrable knowledge of good programming practices including software configuration management. The successful applicant must be able to demonstrate a combination of good analytical and writing skills; proven ability to work both independently and as an integral member of a team; and a proven ability to work to deadlines. Familiarity with some of the commonly used software products (especially a relational database management system such as Rdb or Oracle) and application generators such as RALLY or OracleForms, COBOL or Datatrieve, is essential. Experience in the medical/health care industry would be an asset.

Job Title: *INTERMEDIATE APPLICATIONS PROGRAMMER – MATERIALS MANAGEMENT SYSTEMS*
Department: Systems Development (Materials Management Systems Section)

Duties. Under the general supervision of a Senior Applications Programmer, converts data from project specifications and detailed workflow chart to create or modify computer-integrated purchasing and inventory control programs. Receives from Senior Applications Programmer detailed workflow chart and diagram that illustrates sequence of steps that program must follow and describes input, output, and logical operations involved. Analyzes workflow chart and diagram, applying knowledge of computer capabilities, subject matter, and symbolic logic. Converts detailed logical flow chart to language processable by computer. Supervises entry of program codes into computer system and inputting of test data. Observes computer monitor screen to interpret program operating codes. Corrects program errors, using methods such as modifying program or altering sequence of program steps. Writes program documentation and instructions to guide client personnel in system operations. May direct and coordinate work of Junior Applications Programmers to write, test, and modify computer programs.

Desirable Qualifications. Applicant should have a university degree in Computer Science with a minimum of one year work experience in purchasing/inventory control software, and a demonstrable knowledge of good programming practices including software configuration management. The successful applicant must be able to demonstrate a combination of good analytical and writing skills; proven ability to work both independently and as an integral member of a team; and a proven ability to work to deadlines. Familiarity with some of the commonly used software products (especially a relational database management system such as Rdb or Oracle) and application generators such as RALLY or OracleForms, COBOL or Datatrieve, is essential. Experience in the medical/health care industry would be an asset.

Job Title: *INTERMEDIATE APPLICATIONS PROGRAMMER – MEDICATION TRACKING SYSTEMS*
Department: Systems Development (Medication Tracking Systems Section)

Duties. Under the general supervision of a Senior Applications Programmer, converts data from project specifications and detailed workflow chart to create or modify computer medication tracking programs. Receives from Senior Applications Programmer detailed workflow chart and diagram that illustrates sequence of steps that program must follow and describes input, output, and logical operations involved. Analyzes workflow chart and diagram, applying knowledge of computer capabilities, subject matter, and symbolic logic. Converts detailed logical flow chart to language processable by computer. Supervises entry of program codes into computer system and inputting of test data. Observes computer monitor screen to interpret program operating codes. Corrects program errors, using methods such as modifying program or altering sequence of program steps. Writes program documentation and instructions to guide client personnel in system operations. May direct and coordinate work of Junior Applications Programmers to write, test, and modify computer programs.

Desirable Qualifications. Applicant should have a university degree in Computer Science with a minimum of one year of work experience in medication tracking software, and a demonstrable knowledge of good programming practices including software configuration management. The successful applicant must be able to demonstrate a combination of good analytical and writing skills; proven ability to work both independently and as an integral member of a team; and a proven ability to work to deadlines. Familiarity with some of the commonly used software products (especially a relational database management system such as Rdb or Oracle) and application generators such as RALLY or OracleForms, COBOL or Datatrieve, is essential. Experience in the medical/health care industry would be an asset.

Job Title: *INTERMEDIATE APPLICATIONS PROGRAMMER – RECORDS SYSTEMS*
Department: Systems Development (Record Systems Section)

Duties. Under the general supervision of a Senior Applications Programmer, converts data from project specifications and detailed workflow chart to create or modify computer record-keeping programs. Receives from Senior Applications Programmer detailed workflow chart and diagram that illustrates sequence of steps that program must follow and describes input, output, and logical operations involved. Analyzes workflow chart and diagram, applying knowledge of computer capabilities, subject matter, and symbolic logic. Converts detailed logical flow chart to language processable by computer. Supervises entry of program codes into computer system and inputting of test data. Observes computer monitor screen to interpret program operating codes. Corrects program errors, using methods such as modifying program or altering sequence of program steps. Writes program documentation and instructions to guide client personnel in system operations. May direct and coordinate work of Junior Applications Programmers to write, test, and modify computer programs.

Desirable Qualifications. Applicant should have a university degree in Computer Science with a minimum of one year work experience in record keeping software, and a demonstrable knowledge of good programming practices including software configuration management. The successful applicant must be able to demonstrate a combination of good analytical and writing skills; proven ability to work both independently and as an integral member of a team; and a proven ability to work to deadlines. Familiarity with some of the commonly used software products (especially a relational database management system such as Rdb or Oracle) and application generators such as RALLY or OracleForms, COBOL or Datatrieve, is essential. Experience in the medical/health care industry would be an asset.

Job Title: *INTERMEDIATE APPLICATIONS PROGRAMMER – SCHEDULING SYSTEMS*
Department: Systems Development (Scheduling Systems Section)

Duties. Under the general supervision of a Senior Applications Programmer, converts data from project specifications and detailed workflow chart to create or modify computer-integrated patient, staffing, and facilities scheduling programs. Receives from Senior Applications Programmer detailed workflow chart and diagram that illustrates sequence of steps that program must follow and describes input, output, and logical operations involved. Analyzes workflow chart and diagram, applying knowledge of computer capabilities, subject matter, and symbolic logic. Converts detailed logical flow chart to language processable by computer. Supervises entry of program codes into computer system and inputting of test data. Observes computer monitor screen to interpret program operating codes. Corrects program errors, using methods such as modifying program or altering sequence of program steps. Writes program documentation and instructions to guide client personnel in system operations. May direct and coordinate work of Junior Applications Programmers to write, test, and modify computer programs.

Desirable Qualifications. Applicant should have a university degree in computer science with a minimum of one year work experience in scheduling software, and a demonstrable knowledge of good programming practices including software configuration management. The successful applicant must be able to demonstrate a combination of good analytical and writing skills; proven ability to work both independently and as an integral member of a team; and a proven ability to work to deadlines. Familiarity with some of the commonly used software products (especially a relational database management system such as Rdb or Oracle) and application generators such as RALLY or OracleForms, COBOL or Datatrieve, is essential. Experience in the medical/health care industry would be an asset.

Job Title: *SENIOR APPLICATIONS PROGRAMMER – FINANCIAL MANAGEMENT SYSTEMS*
Department: Systems Development (Financial Management Systems Section)

Duties. Under the direction of the Manager of Financial Management Systems Development, prepares detailed workflow charts and diagrams to illustrate sequence of steps that integrated billing, payments, and financial information program modules must follow and to describe input, output, and logical operations involved, based on workflow charts and contract specifications prepared by the Marketing Department. Confers with supervisor and representatives of Marketing Department to resolve questions of program intent, data input, output requirements, and inclusion of internal checks and controls. Confers with representatives of Systems Integration Section to ensure compatibility of financial systems modules with other modules in project. Supervises conversion of detailed logical flow chart to language processable by computer by intermediate- and junior-level Applications Programmers. Reviews the program testing process, and ensures that program errors have been eliminated. Reviews program documentation and client instructions prepared by Intermediate Applications Programmers. May assist Systems Installation Department in preparation of client training material for financial management system modules.

Desirable Qualifications. Applicant should have a university degree in Computer Science with a minimum of three years of related experience in applications software, with a minimum of one year in financial management software, and demonstrable knowledge of good programming practices including software configuration management. Some course work in accounting principles and practices. The successful applicant must be able to demonstrate a combination of good analytical and writing skills; proven ability to work both independently and as an integral member of a team; and a proven ability to work to deadlines. Familiarity with commonly used software products (especially a relational database management system such as Rdb or Oracle), and with application generators such as RALLY or OracleForms, COBOL or Datatrieve, and general project management skills are essential. Experience in the medical/health care industry would be an asset, as well as experience in supervision and leading project teams.

Job Title: *SENIOR APPLICATIONS PROGRAMMER – MATERIALS MANAGEMENT SYSTEMS*
Department: Systems Development (Materials Management Systems Section)

Duties. Under the direction of the Manager of Materials Management Systems Development, prepares detailed workflow charts and diagrams to illustrate sequence of steps that integrated purchasing and inventory control program modules must follow and to describe input, output, and logical operations involved, based on workflow charts and contract specifications prepared by the

Marketing Department. Confers with supervisor and representatives of Marketing Department to resolve questions of program intent, data input, output requirements, and inclusion of internal checks and controls. Confers with representatives of Systems Integration Section to ensure compatibility of materials management system modules with other modules in project. Supervises conversion of detailed logical flow chart to language processable by computer by intermediate and junior level Applications Programmers. Reviews the program testing process, and ensures that program errors have been eliminated. Reviews program documentation and client instructions prepared by Intermediate Applications Programmers. May assist Systems Installations Department in preparing client training material for materials management modules.

Desirable Qualifications. Applicant should have a university degree in Computer Science with a minimum of three years related experience in applications software with a minimum of one year in materials management software, and demonstrable knowledge of good programming practices including software configuration management. Some course work in purchasing management. The successful applicant must be able to demonstrate a combination of good analytical and writing skills; proven ability to work both independently and as an integral member of a team; and a proven ability to work to deadlines. Familiarity with commonly used software products (especially a relational database management system such as Rdb or Oracle) and with application generators such as RALLY or OracleForms, COBOL or Datatrieve, and general project management skills are essential. Experience in the medical/health care industry would be an asset, as well as experience in supervision and leading project teams.

Job Title: *SENIOR APPLICATIONS PROGRAMMER – MEDICATION TRACKING SYSTEMS*
Department: Systems Development (Medication Tracking Systems Section)

Duties. Under the direction of the Manager of Medication Tracking Systems Development, prepares detailed workflow charts and diagrams to illustrate sequence of steps that medication tracking program modules must follow and to describe input, output, and logical operations involved, based on workflow charts and contract specifications prepared by the Marketing Department. Confers with supervisor and representatives of Marketing Department to resolve questions of program intent, data input, output requirements, and inclusion of internal checks and controls. Confers with representatives of Systems Integration Section to ensure compatibility of medications tracking systems modules with other modules in project. Supervises conversion of detailed logical flow chart to language processable by computer by intermediate- and junior-level Applications Programmers. Reviews the program testing process, and ensures that program errors have been eliminated. Reviews program documentation and client instructions prepared by Intermediate Applications Programmers. May assist Systems Installation Department in preparation of client training material for medication tracking systems modules.

Desirable Qualifications. Applicant should have a university degree in Computer Science with a minimum of three years of related experience in applications software with a minimum of one year in medication tracking software, and demonstrable knowledge of good programming practices including software configuration management. Some course work in pharmacy and drug dispensing principles and practices. The successful applicant must be able to demonstrate a combination of good analytical and writing skills; proven ability to work both independently and as an integral member of a team; and a proven ability to work to deadlines. Familiarity with commonly used software products (especially a relational database management system such as Rdb or Oracle) and with application generators such as RALLY or OracleForms, COBOL or

Datatrieve, and general project management skills are essential. Experience in the medical/health care industry would be an asset, as well as experience in supervision and leading project teams.

Job Title: *SENIOR APPLICATIONS PROGRAMMER – RECORDS SYSTEMS*
Department: Systems Development (Records Systems Section)

Duties. Under the direction of the Manager of Record Systems Development, prepares detailed workflow charts and diagrams to illustrate sequence of steps that record-keeping program modules must follow and to describe input, output, and logical operations involved, based on workflow charts and contract specifications prepared by the Marketing Department. Confers with supervisor and representatives of Marketing Department to resolve questions of program intent, data input, output requirements, and inclusion of internal checks and controls. Confers with representatives of Systems Integration Section to ensure compatibility of records system modules with other modules in project. Supervises conversion of detailed logical flow chart to language processable by computer by intermediate- and junior-level Applications Programmers. Reviews the program testing process, and ensures that program errors have been eliminated. Reviews program documentation and client instructions prepared by Intermediate Applications Programmers. May assist Systems Installation Department in preparation of client training material for record-keeping modules.

Desirable Qualifications. Applicant should have a university degree in Computer Science with a minimum of three years of related experience in applications software with a minimum of one year in record-keeping software, and demonstrable knowledge of good programming practices including software configuration management. Some course work in advanced database management. The successful applicant must be able to demonstrate a combination of good analytical and writing skills; proven ability to work both independently and as an integral member of a team; and a proven ability to work to deadlines. Familiarity with commonly used software products (especially a relational database management system such as Rdb or Oracle) and with application generators such as RALLY or OracleForms, COBOL or Datatrieve, and general project management skills are essential. Experience in the medical/health care industry would be an asset, as well as experience in supervision and leading project teams.

Job Title: *SENIOR APPLICATIONS PROGRAMMER – SCHEDULING SYSTEMS*
Department: Systems Development (Scheduling Systems Section)

Duties. Under the direction of the Manager of Scheduling Systems Development, prepares detailed workflow charts and diagrams to illustrate sequence of steps that patient and employee record-keeping program modules must follow and to describe input, output, and logical operations involved, based on workflow charts and contract specifications prepared by the Marketing Department. Confers with supervisor and representatives of Marketing Department to resolve questions of program intent, data input, output requirements, and inclusion of internal checks and controls. Confers with representatives of Systems Integration Section to ensure compatibility of scheduling systems modules with other modules in project. Supervises conversion of detailed logical flow chart to language processable by computer by intermediate- and junior-level Applications Programmers. Reviews the program testing process, and ensures that program errors have been eliminated. Reviews program documentation and client instructions prepared by Intermediate Applications Programmers. May assist Systems Installation Department in preparation of client training material for scheduling systems modules.

Desirable Qualifications. Applicant should have a university degree in Computer Science with a minimum of three years of related experience in applications software with a minimum of one year in scheduling software, and demonstrable knowledge of good programming practices including software configuration management. Some course work in operations management. The successful applicant must be able to demonstrate a combination of good analytical and writing skills; proven ability to work both independently and as an integral member of a team; and a proven ability to work to deadlines. Familiarity with commonly used software products (especially a relational database management system such as Rdb or Oracle) and with application generators such as RALLY or OracleForms, COBOL or Datatrieve, and general project management skills are essential. Experience in the medical/health care industry would be an asset, as well as experience in supervision and leading project teams.

Job Title: *CARETAKER*
Department: Finance and Administration (Facilities Management Section)

Duties. This person performs cleaning tasks both manually and using industrial-type scrubbing machines, under the general supervision of facilities managers. Duties include cleaning floors of halls, offices, and lavatories, using dry mop, wet mop, and broom. Operating industrial cleaning equipment in stripping, scrubbing, waxing, and polishing floors. Performing such minor repairs as replacing light bulbs, tightening or replacing screws in furniture, and maintaining cleaning equipment. Emptying and cleaning wastepaper baskets. Washing hand basins, toilet bowls, soap dishes, and other washroom equipment, and replenishing supplies of soap, towels, and toilet tissue. Opening and locking buildings at specified times. Moving furniture. Periodically washing walls, ceilings, windows, and doors. Reporting unusual circumstances such as vandalism, theft, and unauthorized persons. Providing all caretaking services as outlined in the *Caretaker Handbook*. Promoting good working relations with staff and customers. Performing related duties as assigned.

Desirable Qualifications. Elementary school education sufficient to provide skill in reading instructions. Good physical condition. Preferably experience in using hand- and power-operated cleaning equipment and cleaning materials.

Job Title: *COMPENSATION CLERK*
Department: Human Resources

Duties. Under the direction of the Compensation Officer, this person performs a variety of moderately complex clerical tasks associated with the compensation function. Although their work is supervised by the Compensation Manager, they are responsible for carrying out a series of clerical assignments without detailed instruction or review. These employees maintain cooperative and helpful relations in their contacts with other staff. Duties include: Setting up files for new employees. Coding and processing Payroll Authorization Forms ensuring that appropriate deductions for benefits, tax, dues, and other factors are made. Overseeing preparation of paycheques or direct deposit of compensation. Creating records of employment for employees who are terminating. Making monthly remittance to the Receiver General, insurance programs, and other bodies. Answering enquiries of the Employment Insurance Commission concerning terminated employees or those on extended leave. Answering questions from employees about their paycheques and referring questions to other departments when appropriate.

Desirable Qualifications. Completion of Grade 12, preferably including or supplemented by courses in bookkeeping and introductory computing, including spreadsheets. Ability to enter data into computer systems accurately. Several years of clerical experience, preferably some of which in a compensation role.

Job Title: *COMPENSATION MANAGER*
Department: Human Resources

Duties. Under the direction of the Director of Human Resources, this position is responsible for managing the operation of the compensation system, including staffing, performance review, training and development of staff, and the hardware and software of computer-based compensation administration system, as well as preparing and revising job descriptions and performing job evaluations. Will be responsible for implementing new compensation policies and monitoring their effectiveness on an ongoing basis, making necessary adjustments, and making recommendations for change. Will assist the Director of Human Resources in evaluating the effectiveness of existing compensation policies and formulating recommendations for change to compensation policies.

Desirable Qualifications. A university degree in Commerce or Business administration with compensation and human resources course work, along with a CHRP (Certified Human Resources Professional) designation. A minimum of five years of experience in compensation administration. Experience which will demonstrate the following skills: ability to relate well with other individuals and perform effective supervision; and excellent organization, analytical, and communication skills. Experience in the computer software industry would be an asset.

Job Title: *COMPENSATION OFFICER*
Department: Human Resources

Duties. Under the direction of the Compensation Manager, this position will be responsible for managing the day-to-day activities relating to the operation of the compensation system and for providing accounting support relating to the processing of base pay, performance pay, and benefits for employees. Will supervise several Compensation Clerks. Will stand in for the Compensation Manager when manager is absent.

Desirable Qualifications. A university degree in Commerce or Business Administration with course work in compensation systems and human resources, a CHRP (Certified Human Resources Professional) designation, and experience that will demonstrate the following skills: ability to deal with moderately complex accounting issues; ability to work with large computer systems in a complex environment; ability to work with electronic spreadsheets; ability to relate well with other individuals and perform effective supervision; and good organization, analytical, and communication skills.

Job Title: *DIRECTOR OF HUMAN RESOURCES*
Department: Human Resources

Duties. Under the general direction of the Vice President of Finance and Administration, ensures the acquisition, training, retention, and motivation of personnel needed by Zenith to achieve its corporate goals. Evaluates human resource management strategy and organization design, and recommends new human resource policies to the executive committee when appropriate. Prepares departmental budget. Responsible for the selection, evaluation, and coaching of subordinate Human Resources managers. Evaluates current policies, procedures, and practices for achieving departmental objectives, and implements improved policies, procedures, and practices. Ensures that company compensation expenditures are deployed effectively. Recommends the most effective compensation and reward strategy and oversees the implementation of approved policies and strategies. Assists other departments in dealing effectively with human resources issues and problems. Provides support to top management in identifying strategic issues and trends affecting the company.

Desirable Qualifications. This position requires a university Commerce or Business Administration degree, with specialization in human resources, as well as additional course work at the post-graduate level, such as a Master of Business Administration with a specialization in human resources, and a CHRP (Certified Human Resources Professional) designation. At least ten years experience in human resource positions, with at least five years in the software industry, and at least five years in a management capacity. Demonstrated ability to coordinate, develop, and supervise staff, deal with individual and group conflict, and meet departmental performance objectives are essential. Excellent verbal and written communications skills. Strong abilities to identify organizational problems and deal with them. Ability to cooperate effectively with and assist managers at a similar organizational level.

Job Title: *DIRECTOR OF MARKETING*
Department: Marketing

Duties. Under the general direction of the Vice President of Finance and Administration, manages the marketing and sales of client systems that meet customer needs and will make a positive contribution to Zenith's financial performance. Evaluates current marketing strategy and recommends new strategy to the executive committee when appropriate. Prepares sales forecasts, and estimated production needs for each fiscal year. Ensures that contracted products will meet customer needs, are costed accurately, and will contribute a satisfactory profit margin to Zenith. Ensures that budgeted sales levels are accomplished. Prepares departmental budget. Evaluates current policies, procedures, and practices for achieving departmental objectives, and implements improved policies, procedures, and practices. In conjunction with the Human Resources Department, responsible for selection, evaluation, and coaching of regional managers. Liaises with other Department Managers to ensure that overall corporate and systems objectives are being accomplished. Provides support to top management in identifying strategic issues and trends affecting the company.

Desirable Qualifications. This position requires a university Commerce or Business Administration degree, with specialization in marketing, as well as additional marketing course work at the post-graduate level, such as a Master of Business Administration with a specialization in marketing. At least ten years of experience in marketing/sales of applications software, with at least five years in a management capacity. Sufficient course work/work experience in computing science to understand the principles, processes, and practices of systems charting. Demonstrated ability to coordinate, develop, and supervise staff, deal with individual and group conflict, and meet departmental deadlines and performance objectives are essential. Excellent verbal and written communications skills. At least two years of experience in applications software for medical/health care industry. Strong abilities to identify organizational problems and deal with them. Ability to cooperate effectively with managers at a similar organizational level.

Job Title: *DIRECTOR OF SYSTEMS DEVELOPMENT*
Department: Systems Development

Duties. Under the general direction of the Vice President of Systems, manages the development of client systems that meet contract specifications, budgeted costs, and production deadlines. Prepares departmental budget. Evaluates current policies, procedures, and practices for achieving departmental objectives, and implements improved policies, procedures, and practices. In conjunction with the Human Resources Department, responsible for selection, evaluation, and coaching of section managers. Liaises with other Department Managers to ensure that overall corporate and systems objectives are being accomplished. Provides support to top management in identifying strategic issues and trends affecting the company.

Desirable Qualifications. This position requires a university Computing Science degree, as well as a Commerce or Business Administration degree or Master of Business Administration degree, and at least ten years experience in managing applications software design. Demonstrated ability to coordinate, develop, and supervise staff, deal with individual and group conflict, and meet departmental deadlines and performance objectives are essential. Excellent verbal and written communications skills. At least two years of experience in applications software for medical/health care industry. Strong abilities to identify organizational problems and deal with them. Ability to cooperate effectively with managers at a similar organizational level.

Job Title: *MANAGER OF FINANCIAL SYSTEMS DEVELOPMENT*
Department: Systems Development (Financial Systems Section)

Duties. Under the direction of the Director of Systems Development, coordinates the preparation of financial systems modules that meet contract specifications. In cooperation with the Systems Integration Section, ensures that the completed module integrates with and is fully compatible with other client system modules. Monitors and analyzes the performance of the section relative to budgeted project costs and timelines. Evaluates current procedures and practices for achieving section objectives, and implements improved procedures and practices. In conjunction with the Human Resources Department, responsible for selection of section staff, promotion, discharge, or transfer. Oversees training, development, and coordination of staff, and deals effectively with any conflict management issues that arise.

Desirable Qualifications. This position requires a university Computing Science degree, supplemented by specific course work in financial and accounting systems. An accounting designation would normally be required, although an equivalent combination of training and experience may be considered. At least three years of work experience in financial systems and three years in other applications systems. Demonstrated abilities to coordinate and supervise staff, deal with individual and group conflict, and meet deadlines are essential. Good verbal and written communications skills. Experience in the medical/health care industry is an asset.

Job Title: *REGIONAL MARKETING MANAGER*
Department: Marketing

Duties. Under the general direction of the Director of Marketing, manages the marketing and sales of client systems that meet customer needs and will make a positive contribution to Zenith's financial performance for a given region. Prepares regional sales forecasts. Ensures that contracted products will meet customer needs, that product specifications are well developed, and that product costing is accurate. In conjunction with marketing policies, sets a price for the product that will contribute a satisfactory profit margin to Zenith. May get involved in client negotiations over price or product design issues. Approves all product proposals and contracts, subject to final review by Director of Marketing. Ensures that budgeted sales levels are accomplished. Prepares regional budget. Evaluates current policies, procedures, and practices for achieving regional objectives, and implements improved policies, procedures, and practices. Responsible for selection, evaluation, coaching, promotion, transfer, or discharge of Systems Marketing Specialists and Systems Design Analysts. Jointly with Regional Maintenance Manager, oversees administration of the regional office.

Desirable Qualifications. This position requires a university Commerce or Business Administration degree, with specialization in marketing. At least three to five years of experience in marketing/sales of medical/health care applications software. Sufficient course work (or work experience) in computing science to understand the principles, processes, and practices of systems charting. Demonstrated ability to coordinate, develop, and supervise staff, deal with interpersonal conflict, and meet departmental deadlines and performance objectives are essential. Excellent verbal and written communications skills.

Job Title: *SECRETARY*
Departments: All

Duties. These individuals provide secretarial and administrative support to Directors and Managers, and perform responsible, varied, and complex clerical tasks. The assignments typically require the use of a broad understanding of the structure and division of responsibility, and functions of the units they service. Expected to take initiative in relieving Directors/Managers of administrative detail that does not require the application of professional judgement. This may involve drafting letters and maintaining records on budget allotments, expenditures, commitments, and residual balances. Screening of phone and office calls, setting up appointments, answering questions, and referring visitors to appropriate individuals.

Desirable Qualifications. Grade 12 plus completion of secretarial/administrative assistant training program, with working knowledge of word processing, spreadsheet, and related programs. Excellent verbal and written communication skills. A minimum of two years of workplace experience.

Job Title: *SYSTEMS DESIGN ANALYST*
Department: Marketing

Duties. Under the direction of the Regional Marketing Manager, this person analyzes client requirements, procedures, and problems to provide effective computer solutions. Confers with Systems Marketing Specialist and with personnel of client units to analyze current operational procedures, identify problems, and learn specific input and output requirements, such as forms of data input, how data is to be summarized, and formats for reports. Writes detailed description of user needs, program functions, and steps required to develop or modify computer systems. Reviews computer functions, and steps required to develop or modify computer program. Reviews computer system capabilities, workflow, and scheduling limitations to determine if requested program or program change is possible within existing system. Prepares workflow charts and diagrams to specify in detail operations to be performed by computer system. Prepares time and cost estimates for projects, along with proposal specifications and/or contract specifications.

Desirable Qualifications. This position requires a university degree in Computer Science, and a minimum of three years experience with various applications systems. The successful applicant will have a good understanding of hardware capacities, large area networks, servers, the Internet and Internet tools, and all operating systems. Other qualifications include: excellent verbal communication skills and excellent written communications skills; the ability to work independently; excellent charting and workflow analysis abilities; the ability to estimate and segment project requirements accurately; and the ability to establish effective communication and relationships with client personnel in a short time frame.

Job Title: *SENIOR SYSTEMS HARDWARE ANALYST*
Department: Systems Installations

Duties. Under the general direction of the Director of Systems Installation, analyzes requirements of the client software produced by Systems Development in order to determine hardware that will provide system capabilities required for projected workloads, and plans hardware layout of the new system. Confers with client project managers to obtain information on limitations and capabilities of existing hardware and capabilities required for the contracted system and projected workload. Evaluates factors such as number of departments serviced by computing equipment, reporting formats required, volume of transactions, time requirements and cost constraints, and need for security and access restrictions to determine hardware configurations. Analyzes information to determine, recommend, and plan layout for type of computers and peripheral equipment, or modifications to existing equipment and system, that will provide capability for the contracted software, efficient operation, and effective use of allotted space. May specify power supply requirements and configuration. May recommend purchase of equipment to control dust, temperature, and humidity in area of system installation. Works with client managers to secure agreement on hardware requirements, and prepares documentation on hardware needs and configuration.

Desirable Qualifications. This position requires a university degree in Computer Science, with post-graduate training in hardware and systems engineering, and a minimum of three years of related work experience. The successful applicant will have an understanding of hardware capacities, large area networks, servers, the Internet and Internet tools, and all current desktop operating systems. Other qualifications include: excellent verbal communications skills and excellent written communications skills; the ability to work independently; a high customer service orientation, demonstrated by an ability to establish effective client relations under pressure.

Job Title: *SYSTEMS INTEGRATION SPECIALIST*
Department: Systems Development (Systems Integration Section)

Duties. Under the general direction of the Manager of Systems Integration, coordinates the development of applications modules that will interface effectively to result in an efficient integrated system. Interprets the contract specifications, and in conjunction with applications programmers for each application module, plans compatible and efficient interfaces. Subsequent to completion of all contracted modules and the necessary interfaces, tests the system to make sure it fulfils contract specifications and integrated elements interface effectively. If it does not so, prepares recommended solutions, to be implemented by the applications development departments.

Desirable Qualifications. This position requires a university degree in Computing Science, and work experience in all five types of application systems modules produced by the company. A total of at least five years of work experience in these applications is required, along with extensive course work in systems integration. Other qualifications include: excellent verbal communications skills in group situations and excellent written communications skills; the ability to work collaboratively in a team environment; the ability to provide quality control of services; a high customer service orientation; and an ability to perform effectively under short timelines and other pressures.

Job Title: *SENIOR SYSTEMS INSTALLATION SPECIALIST*
Department: Systems Installations

Duties. Under the general direction of the Director of Systems Installation, coordinates the installation of computer operating system and applications software and tests software operation. Reads loading and running instructions for system and applications software, such as task scheduling, memory management, computer file system, or controlling computer input and output, and loads tape into tape drive or transfers software to magnetic disk. Initiates tests of systems and applications programs and module interfaces, and observes readout on monitor of computer system to detect errors or work stoppage. Enters code changes into computer system to correct errors. Analyzes performance indicators, such as system response time, number of transactions per second, and number of programs being processed at once, to ensure that system is operating efficiently. Changes system software so that system performance will meet objectives. Writes description of steps taken to modify system and procedures required to implement new software. Participates in the supervision and training of less senior systems installations specialists.

Desirable Qualifications. This position requires a university degree in Computer Science, and a minimum of three years of systems installation experience. The successful applicant will have an understanding of, and experience in using, Knowlex's IKnow knowledge database, large area networks, servers, the Internet and Internet tools, and both Windows and Macintosh desktop operating systems. Other qualifications include: excellent verbal communications skills in group situations and excellent written communications skills; the ability to work both independently and collaboratively in a team environment; the ability to provide quality control of services; and a high customer service orientation, demonstrated by an ability to establish and maintain effective client relations under pressure. Good conflict management skills, experience on a project team, and experience in training would be assets.

Job Title: *SYSTEMS MARKETING SPECIALIST*
Department: Marketing

Duties. Under the direction of the Regional Marketing Manager, this person will be responsible for analyzing client needs and recommending appropriate computer solutions to clients; establishing and maintaining good working relationships with customers; disseminating information to clients or software products available from the company; planning marketing promotions; setting up demonstration hardware and operating systems; applications troubleshooting; and maintaining customer satisfaction. Will assist Systems Design Analysts in developing specific systems specifications both at the proposal stage and after a purchase contract has been signed.

Desirable Qualifications. A university degree in Commerce or Business Administration with a marketing concentration. A working knowledge of the operating system and applications software for Windows, DOS, and Macintosh environments; a high customer service orientation; demonstrated interpersonal skills such as the ability to establish equitable working relationships with staff and clients under pressure; demonstrated skills at collaborating with computer professionals to resolve complex problems and identify client needs; demonstrated oral and written communication skills such as the proven ability to determine clients' needs, communicate solutions, answer client support questions, and respond to client requests with minimal supervision. Assets include a demonstrated ability to work independently and in a team as well as experience in working with the medical or health care community.

Job Title: *JUNIOR SYSTEMS TRAINER*
Department: Systems Installations (Systems Training Section)

Duties. Under the supervision of senior systems training staff, assists in preparing training materials and conducting training sessions for client personnel subsequent to system installations. May liaise with other company personnel to obtain source material for preparation of training package.

Desirable Qualifications. A university degree in a behaviourally related field, such as psychology, education, or commerce, with excellent interpersonal, verbal, and written communications skills. Demonstrated ability to organize and make effective presentations. Some demonstrated facility with computer usage. Experience in the medical/health care industry is an asset.

Phase I – Formulating the Compensation Strategy

In Phase I, you need to identify the underlying organizational factors causing the problems at your client firm, provide solutions to these problems, develop an effective reward and compensation strategy, develop and apply a job evaluation plan, and develop a pay-for-knowledge plan.

To successfully accomplish Phase I, you will need to have read and have utilized appropriate concepts from Chapters 1 to 8. When preparing your report, please use the following five main headings.

Phase I Report Headings

Section A: Identification of Current Organizational Problems. In this section, you need to identify the underlying strategic and structural factors (including the reward and compensation system) that are causing the problems that your client is experiencing. Use of key concepts from Chapter 1, application of the strategic framework in Chapter 2, and application of the behavioural framework in Chapter 3 are all essential in so doing. Your entire project rests on this foundation.

Section B: Strategic and Structural Recommendations. Describe the proposed strategic and structural solutions that flow from your analysis in the previous section. Be specific in explaining what you would do. For example, if you think a different managerial strategy is required, exactly what would you do to implement that? If you think some jobs need redesign, which jobs and exactly how should they be changed? You also need to provide a new job description for any redesigned or combined jobs. If you think teams are needed, who would be the team members, and what would be their responsibilities?

Section C: Reward and Compensation Strategy. Next, develop your reward and compensation strategy by following the first four steps in Figure 6.1. You need to define the type of employee behaviour that your client firm needs, define the role that compensation will play in producing these behaviours, determine the compensation mix, and determine the compensation level.

If different behaviours are required from different job families, then this process will need to be repeated for each job family. The outcome of all this should be summarized for each job family in a compensation strategy template (shown on the following page). All jobs listed on the same compensation strategy template will have the same mix of compensation elements and the same compensation level relative to the market (i.e., lag the market by a certain percentage, lead the market by a certain percentage, or match the market). Note, however, that this does *not* mean that all jobs on the same template will receive the same *dollar* amount of pay; it just means they are all subject to the same compensation *strategy*. Figure 6.2 provides an example of a filled-in compensation strategy template. You should carefully read the example that surrounds Figure 6.2.

You will need at least two compensation strategy templates—one for those jobs you are putting under a pay-for-knowledge system (PKS), and at least one for the jobs you will be putting under a job evaluation (JE) system. (You will not be putting any jobs under market pricing.) In fact, it is likely you will need three or four templates for your JE jobs. Every job listed in the "partial listing

Compensation Strategy Template

Jobs Covered: _____

Total Compensation Level: Match? _____ **OR** Lead? _____% **OR** Lag? _____%

Compensation Component	Projected Proportion of Total Compensation
1. Base Pay	%
a. Job Evaluation	%
b. Market Pricing	%
c. Pay for Knowledge	%
2. Performance Pay	%
a. Individual Performance Pay	%
i. Piece Rates	%
ii. Commissions	%
iii. Merit Bonuses	%
iv. Special Incentives	%
b. Group Performance Pay	%
i. Gain Sharing	%
ii. Goal Sharing	%
iii. Other Group Pay	%
c. Organization Performance Pay	%
i. Profit Sharing	%
ii. Stock Plan	%
iii. Other Organization Pay	%
3. Indirect Pay	%
i. Mandatory Benefits	%
ii. Retirement Income (Pension Plan)	%
iii. Health Benefits	%
iv. Paid Time Off	%
v. Employee Services	%
vi. Other Benefits	%

of job descriptions" at the end of your client description must appear on a compensation strategy template (except for any jobs you may eliminate by job redesign). For any new jobs that you create, you must prepare a job description, and that job must appear on a compensation strategy template.

In creating job families, the first thing to decide is which jobs will be included under the pay-for-knowledge system. (Material in Chapter 4 will be useful in making this decision.) The remaining jobs will fall under job evaluation, and you need to consider how many distinct groupings of behaviours (job families) that you should have. (Incidentally, you do not need to include top management—the CEO and the two Vice Presidents—in a job family. Those three jobs will not be included in your compensation system.)

Bear in mind that creating a high number of job families creates a very complex compensation structure, but that too few job families may result in an inappropriate compensation strategy for some jobs. In this case, less than three JE job families is likely too few, while more than five JE job families is probably too many.

To successfully complete this section, you will need to utilize the concepts contained in Chapters 4, 5, and 6. The quality of this section (and the mark you receive for it) depends on how well you can demonstrate application of these concepts. Incidentally, don't forget to include the behavioural objectives you are setting for the compensation system (see Table 6.2).

Section D: Job Evaluation Plan. In this section you should describe your job evaluation plan, which should be constructed using the "Point Method" (see Chapter 8). You need to describe the compensable factors you have selected, the factor definitions you have developed, the factor scales you are using, and the factor weights you are applying, along with your rationale for all this.

As a part of this, you need to construct a summary rating chart similar to that shown in Figure 8.1, and then apply the job evaluation system to each of the jobs being evaluated, so that there is a point total for each job. Use a table similar to Table 8.2 to display the results of this, in which the scores for each factor are shown for each job, and the jobs are ranked from highest points total to lowest.

In completing this section, you should cover everything in Chapter 8 except the three sections on "Testing for Market Fit," "Exploring for Solutions to Job Evaluation Problems," and "Testing for Total Compensation Costs." (These issues will be covered in Phase II.) You should also have read Chapter 7, as background to put the material in Chapter 8 into context.

Section E: Pay-for-Knowledge Plan. The final section should describe your pay-for-knowledge plan, including the skill blocks you have chosen, in the form of a skill grid similar to that in Table 4.1. You need to deal with all of the "Issues in Developing a Skill-Based Pay System" (as described in Chapter 4), except deciding whom to include in the PKS (you explained that in Section C), and pricing the skill blocks, which you will do in Phase II.

Format and Organization of Report

The best format for the submission of your report is a three-ring binder, with tabs indicating each of the five main sections in Phase I. Additional headings should be used within each of the main sections. Don't use appendices; include all relevant material for each section within that section. Include a detailed table of contents, which you will update as Phases II and III are added to the report. Reports must be typed, double-spaced, with a 12-point font and one-inch margins.

Grading Criteria

In addition to the quality of work, application of concepts, and insights shown in Sections A to E of your report, other grading criteria include the organization of the report, the clarity of expression, the format, and the integration/coherence of the report. Be sure that each section is consistent with and follows from previous sections, and that excess repetition is avoided. Ten percent of your project grade is reserved for the presentation that is made on the submission date.

One final item to be included with your report is an appraisal of the performance of each group member, based on a comprehensive and fair performance appraisal system. (Use concepts from Chapter 10 to help develop this.) This should include a sheet as shown in the course outline, showing the grade distribution across team members for Phase I. (No more than two team members can receive the exact same grade allocation.) The quality of your team member performance appraisal system is a grading factor.

Phase II – Aligning the Compensation System with the Market

In Phase II, your task is to calibrate your compensation system to the market, by creating a pay structure that flows from the compensation strategy, job evaluation plan, and pay-for-knowledge plan that you developed in Phase I. The end result will be a pay structure that provides a pay range —including the projected dollar amounts of base pay, performance pay, and indirect pay—for every job at your client firm (all those for which you have a job description).

In preparing Phases II and III of your report, you will use a software package called "CompSoft" to access the necessary data and to help you do some of the necessary calculations. Bear in mind that "CompSoft" does not design a compensation system for you; it simply helps with the mechanical aspects. Do not get lost in the software—the key is to *understand the underlying basis* for each of the steps in the software. *Remember, your goal in this class is to learn how to design effective compensation systems, not how to do simulations!* The simulation will only be a meaningful learning experience for you if you first absorb the relevant concepts from the text and your classes.

To successfully accomplish Phase II, you will need to have read and have utilized appropriate concepts from Chapters 7 to 9 and the "Pricing the Skill Blocks" section of Chapter 4. Use the following five headings for Phase II, utilizing the same letters for your tabs.

Phase II Report Headings

Section F: Design of Compensation Survey. CompSoft includes compensation survey results for selected jobs at a sample of 24 Canadian firms. Your task in this section is to select, and justify, the specific firms to use as appropriate comparators to calibrate your pay system to the market.

Factors to consider in selecting these "market comparator firms" include similarities in the labour market (do we compete for the same type of employees?), similarities in the product market (do we compete for the same customers?), geographic locale (do we compete for employees in the same regions?) and company size (do we have a similar size of firm?). The idea here is to select enough comparator firms to get a representative and reliable sample, while excluding firms that are not good comparators for your client firm. Chapter 9 provides the foundation for this section.

In this case, selecting fewer than eight firms is unlikely to produce valid results, while selecting more than ten firms *may* indicate inclusion of some inappropriate comparators, depending on how you have balanced your sample. Be sure to explain a detailed rationale for your selection process! A table of how each possible market comparator stands on each of your selection criteria would be helpful in describing your rationale. Include a printout of Screen 1 in this section of your report.

Section G: Identification of Benchmark Jobs. In this section, you identify the benchmark jobs you will use in calibrating your job evaluation system to the market. You need to select four or five jobs (three is the absolute minimum) from the compensation survey that are equivalent to jobs included in your job evaluation structure. You should try to find market matches for a job to which you gave a low job evaluation point total (from your work in Phase I), one with a high JE point total, and two or three jobs in between. Explain your rationale for the jobs you select. The section "Testing the Job Evaluation System" in Chapter 8 discusses this issue.

It is crucial that the market comparator jobs you select from the compensation survey are truly equivalent to the matching benchmark jobs at your client firm. If they are not good matches, your entire compensation system will fail! Be sure to look at more than the job titles when making your choices. Compare the job descriptions carefully, and utilize the "Job Description Trailers" to help you make your choices. Include printouts of Screens 3 and 4 in this section of your report.

Section H: Development of Job Evaluation Pay Structure. Once you have selected your benchmark jobs, it is time to test your job evaluation system. This is done by relating JE points to dollars, through the creation of a "market line," as discussed in Chapter 8. You need to decide whether to use "average mean total compensation" as your measure or "weighted average mean total compensation" as your measure, and explain why you made the choice you did. You may also want to do some analysis of the market data for your market comparator jobs (see Chapter 9 for information on analyzing market data).

This market line and the accompanying correlation (regression) coefficient (R^2) give an indication of whether your job evaluation system may have problems, as discussed in Chapter 8. Be sure to examine the outliers and the slope of the line, in addition to the correlation coefficient, as discussed in Chapter 8. If there are problems, there are many possible causes, and it is essential to explore these and come up with solutions before proceeding. Include this discussion in your paper and your solutions, if needed. You need to take the time to get your market line right, because everything that follows from this point depends on the creation of a satisfactory market line.

Once you are confident that you have a satisfactory market line, the next step is to create a pay policy line. However, you should do this only if you have selected the same overall compensation level policy for all the jobs in your job evaluation system. An example of using the same compensation *level* policy is where you would lead the market by 5% in total compensation for all jobs in your JE system. (You can have different compensation *mix* policies, however.) If you have different compensation level policies for your different JE families (or if you choose to match the market in total compensation for all your JE jobs), then your market line will serve as your pay policy line, and you will make the necessary adjustments to compensation level in Screen 8.

Your next task is to create a pay structure with pay grades and ranges. This is based on the section entitled "Determining the Base Pay Structure" in Chapter 8. Apply everything in that section, explaining your actions at every step.

Once you have created your pay structure, you need to slot all your JE jobs into the appropriate pay grades (this is done in Screen 9). Then, apply the compensation mix proportions from the compensation strategy templates that you prepared in Phase I, to produce the base pay ranges, performance pay ranges, and indirect pay ranges for each job. *Note that this process should be done for all jobs included in your job evaluation pay structure, not just your benchmark jobs!* Screen 9 is the most important output from Phase II, and provides the foundation for Phase III.

In this section of your report, include printouts of Screens 5, 6, 7, 8, and 9, as well as your market line graph, pay policy graph, and pay structure graph.

Section I: Conducting and Managing the Job Evaluation Process. In this section, describe how you would handle the issues involved in conducting and managing the job evaluation process, as discussed in Chapter 7.

Section J: Pay-for-Knowledge Pay Structure. In this section, use the high-low method to establish the entry-level and top-level total compensation amounts in your skill grid, and for pricing your skill blocks (see the "Pricing the Skill Blocks" section of Chapter 4). To do so, you will need to use the market data included in CompSoft. Use the same market sample of companies that you selected earlier for your job evaluation analysis (but of course you will not use the same benchmark jobs that you used for job evaluation).

You will need to pick a market comparator job from the compensation data that matches the skills required at the "top level" of your pay-for-knowledge system, and one that matches the "entry level" of your PKS. (To actually get the total market compensation for these two market comparator jobs, the software will require you to enter three jobs. Pick any other job and include it, but ignore the results for that job.) As is necessary for all sections of your report, be sure to provide your rationale for everything you do, and carefully explain the basis for your calculations.

Once you have the total compensation levels for your high and your low jobs, you do not use CompSoft any further for your pay-for-knowledge system. If you are applying a lead or a lag strategy to your PKS jobs, adjust the total compensation for your high-low jobs accordingly. As explained in Chapter 4, calculate the actual dollar amounts (in terms of total compensation) for each skill block, and put them right on your skill grid. Include a copy of your priced skill grid here. Also in this section, be sure to include your entry level compensation and your top level compensation, including a breakdown of base pay, performance pay, and indirect pay, based on your compensation strategy template for your PKS jobs.

Jobs Included in the Compensation Survey

Following are the jobs for which market data have been collected through a compensation survey. The job descriptions for these jobs (adapted from the *Dictionary of Occupational Titles*) start on page 62 of this manual. Examine these job descriptions carefully to find jobs that are equivalent to those in your job evaluation structure at your client firm. (The jobs from the market data are known as "market comparator jobs" while the matching jobs from your client firm are known as "benchmark jobs.") You also need to find a "high" job match and a "low" job match for your pay-for-knowledge system. *Note that jobs with similar job titles to those at your client firm may not necessarily be truly equivalent.* Use the job definition trailers to help you decide.

Accountant, Tax

Clerk, Accounting

Clerk, Administrative

Clerk, General

Clerk, Sales

Computer Programmer

Janitor

Manager, Department

Manager, Engineering, Electronics

Manager, General

Manager, Office

Manager, Sales

Personnel Recruiter

Programmer/Analyst

Sales Representative, Commercial Products/Services

Secretary

Supervisor, Technical Services, Electrical Machinery

Systems Analyst

Systems Programmer

Technical Support Specialist

Technician, Apprentice, Electrical Machinery

Training Officer

Components of the Job Description Trailer

At the end of each job description listed on pages 62 to 70, you will see a "trailer" with two sets of codes. The first set is the "GED," which is the "General Educational Development" that is deemed necessary to perform the job satisfactorily. The second set is the "SVP" ("Specific Vocational Preparation"), which is the amount of time required to gain the knowledge and experience necessary to do the job satisfactorily (the time required for general education is not included in this). Both of these codes are defined below. They are useful in helping to understand whether the jobs in the compensation survey are truly equivalent to the benchmark jobs at your client firm that you have selected for calibrating your job evaluation system, and to the high-low jobs you have selected for calibrating your pay-for-knowledge system.

"General Educational Development" embraces those aspects of education (formal and informal) that are required of the worker for satisfactory job performance. This is education of a general nature that does not have a recognized, specific occupational objective. Ordinarily, such education is obtained in elementary school, high school, or university, although it may be obtained from experience and self-study.

The GED Scale is composed of three divisions: Reasoning Development, Mathematical Development, and Language Development. At the end of each job description, you will see a code that may look like this: GED: R4 M3 L3. What this means is that the job to which this code is attached (Clerk, Accounting) requires a reasoning level of "4," a mathematical level of "3," and a language level of "3." The following are the definitions for each level of the three abilities.

GED – REASONING DEVELOPMENT

R1: Apply common sense understanding to carry out simple one- or two-step instructions. Deal with standardized situations with occasional or no variables in situations encountered on the job.

R2: Apply common sense understanding to carry out detailed but uninvolved written or oral instructions. Deal with problems involving a few concrete variables in standardized situations.

R3: Apply common sense understanding to carry out instructions furnished in written, oral, or diagrammatic form. Deal with problems involving several concrete variables in standardized situations.

R4: Apply principles of rational systems to solve practical problems and deal with a variety of concrete variables in situations where only limited standardization exists. Interpret a variety of instructions furnished in written, oral, diagrammatic, or schedule form. (Examples of rational systems include: bookkeeping, electric wiring systems, house building, farm management, and navigation.)

R5: Apply principles of logical or scientific thinking to define problems, collect data, establish facts, and draw valid conclusions. Interpret an extensive variety of technical instructions in mathematical or diagrammatic form. Deal with several abstract and concrete variables.

R6: Apply principles of logical or scientific thinking to a wide range of intellectual and practical problems. Deal with nonverbal symbolism (formulas, scientific equations, graphs, musical notes, etc.) in its most difficult phases. Deal with a variety of abstract and concrete variables. Apprehend the most abstruse classes of concepts.

GED – MATHEMATICAL DEVELOPMENT

M1: Add and subtract two digit numbers. Multiply and divide 10s and 100s by 2, 3, 4, 5. Perform the four basic arithmetic operations with coins as part of a dollar. Perform operations with units such as cup, pint, and quart; inch, foot, and yard; and ounce and pound.

M2: Add, subtract, multiply, and divide all units of measure. Perform the four operations with like common and decimal fractions. Compute ratio, rate, and percent. Draw and interpret bar graphs. Perform arithmetic operations involving all American monetary units.

M3: Compute discount, interest, profit and loss; commission, markup, and selling price; ratio and proportion; and percentage. Calculate surfaces, volumes, weights, and measures. Algebra: Calculate variables and formulas; monomials and polynomials; ratio and proportion variables; and square roots and radicals. Geometry: Calculate plane and solid figures; circumference, area, and volume. Understand kinds of angles and properties of pairs of angles.

M4: Algebra: Deal with system of real numbers; linear, quadratic, rational, exponential, logarithmic, angle and circular functions, and inverse functions; related algebraic solution of equations and inequalities; limits and continuity; and probability and statistical inference. Geometry: Deductive axiomatic geometry, plane and solid, and rectangular coordinates. Shop Math: Practical application of fractions, percentages, ratio and proportion, measurement, logarithms, slide rule, practical algebra, geometric construction, and essentials of trigonometry.

M5: Algebra: Work with exponents and logarithms, linear equations, quadratic equations, mathematical induction and binomial theorem, and permutations. Calculus: Apply concepts of analytic geometry, differentiations, and integration of algebraic functions with applications. Statistics: Apply mathematical operations to frequency distributions, reliability and validity of tests, normal curve, analysis of variance, correlation techniques, chi-square application and sampling theory, and factor analysis.

M6: Advanced calculus: Work with limits, continuity, real number systems, mean value theorems, and implicit functions theorems. Modern Algebra: Apply fundamental concepts of theories of groups, rings, and fields. Work with differential equations, linear algebra, infinite series, advanced operations methods, and functions of real and complex variables. Statistics: Work with mathematical statistics, mathematical probability and applications, experimental design, statistical inference, and econometrics.

GED – LANGUAGE DEVELOPMENT

L1: Reading: Recognize meaning of 2,500 (two- or three-syllable) words. Read at rate of 95–120 words per minute. Compare similarities and differences between words and between series of numbers. Writing: Print simple sentences containing subject, verb, and object, and series of numbers, names, and addresses. Speaking: Speak simple sentences, using normal word order, and present and past tenses.

L2: Reading: Passive vocabulary of 5,000–6,000 words. Read at rate of 190–215 words per minute. Read adventure stories and comic books, looking up unfamiliar words in dictionary for meaning, spelling, and pronunciation. Read instructions for assembling model cars and airplanes. Writing: Write compound and complex sentences, using cursive style, proper end punctuation, and employing adjectives and adverbs. Speaking: Speak clearly and distinctly with appropriate pauses and emphasis, correct pronunciation, variations in word order, using present, perfect, and future tenses.

L3: Reading: Read a variety of novels, magazines, atlases, and encyclopaedias. Read safety rules, instructions in the use and maintenance of shop tools and equipment, and methods and procedures in mechanical drawing and layout work. Writing: Write reports and essays with proper format, punctuation, spelling, and grammar, using all parts of speech. Speaking: Speak before an audience with poise, voice control, and confidence, using correct English and well-modulated voice.

L4: Reading: Read novels, poems, newspapers, periodicals, journals, manuals, dictionaries, thesauruses, and encyclopaedias. Writing: Prepare business letters, expositions, summaries, and reports, using prescribed format and conforming to all rules of punctuation, grammar, diction, and style. Speaking: Participate in panel discussions, dramatizations, or debates. Speak extemporaneously on varied subjects.

L5: Reading: Read literature, book and play reviews, scientific and technical journals, abstracts, financial reports, and legal documents. Writing: Write novels, plays, editorials, journals, speeches, manuals, critiques, poetry, and songs. Speaking: Conversant in the theory, principles, and methods of effective and persuasive speaking, voice and diction, phonetics, and discussion and debate.

SPECIFIC VOCATIONAL PREPARATION (SVP)

"Specific Vocational Preparation" is defined as the amount of lapsed time required by a typical worker to learn the techniques, acquire the information, and develop the facility needed for average performance in a specific job-worker situation.

This training may be acquired in a vocational school, work, military, institutional, or vocational environment. It does not include the orientation time required of a fully qualified worker to become accustomed to the special conditions of any new job. Specific vocational training includes: vocational education, apprenticeship training, in-plant classroom training, on-the-job training, and essential experience in other jobs. *It does not include years of university training, if any, required to qualify for the job.* The codes for the various levels of specific vocational preparation are as follows:

SVP 1: Short demonstration only
SVP 2: Anything beyond short demonstration up to and including 1 month
SVP 3: Over 1 month up to and including 3 months
SVP 4: Over 3 months up to and including 6 months
SVP 5: Over 6 months up to and including 1 year
SVP 6: Over 1 year up to and including 2 years
SVP 7: Over 2 years up to and including 4 years
SVP 8: Over 4 years up to and including 10 years
SVP 9: Over 10 years

Note: These do not include years of university education, if any, required for the job.

Descriptions for Jobs Included in Compensation Survey

Accountant, Tax

Prepares federal, provincial, or local tax returns of individual, business establishment, or other organization: Examines accounts and records and computes taxes owed according to prescribed rates, laws, and regulations, using computer. Advises management regarding effects of business activities on taxes, and on strategies for minimizing tax liability. Ensures that establishment complies with periodic tax payment, information reporting, and other taxing authority requirements. Represents principal before taxing bodies. May devise and install tax record systems. May specialize in various aspects of tax accounting, such as tax laws applied to particular industry, or in individual, fiduciary, or partnership income tax preparation.   GED: R5 M5 L5. SVP: 8.

Clerk, Accounting

Performs any combination of the following calculating, posting, and verifying duties to obtain financial data for use in maintaining accounting records: Compiles and sorts documents, such as invoices and cheques, substantiating business transactions. Verifies and posts details of business transactions, such as funds received and disbursed, and totals accounts, using calculator or computer. Computes and records charges, refunds, cost of lost or damaged goods, freight charges, rentals, and similar items. May compute wages, taxes, premiums, commissions, and payments. May type vouchers, invoices, cheques, account statements, reports, and other records. May reconcile bank statements. May be designated according to type of accounting performed, such as Accounts-Payable Clerk (clerical); Accounts-Receivable Clerk (clerical); Payroll Clerk; Bill-Recapitulation Clerk (utilities); Rent and Miscellaneous Remittance Clerk (insurance); Tax-Record Clerk (utilities).
GED: R4 M3 L3. SVP: 5.

Clerk, Administrative

Compiles and maintains records of business transactions and office activities of establishment, performing variety of the following or similar clerical duties and utilizing knowledge of systems or procedures: Copies data and compiles records and reports.

Tabulates and posts data in record books. Records orders for merchandise or service. Gives information to and interviews customers, claimants, employees, and sales personnel. Receives, counts, and pays out cash. Prepares, issues, and sends out receipts, bills, policies, invoices, statements, and cheques. Prepares stock inventory. Adjusts complaints. Operates office machines, such as typewriter, adding, calculating, and duplicating machines. Opens and routes incoming mail, answers correspondence, and prepares outgoing mail. May take dictation. May greet and assist visitors. May keep books. May purchase supplies. May operate computer terminal to input and retrieve data. May be designated according to field of activity, such as Adjustment Clerk (retail trade; tel. & tel.); Airport Clerk (air trans.); Colliery Clerk (mine & quarry); Claims Clerk (insurance); Shop Clerk (clerical). GED: R4 M3 L3. SVP: 4.

Clerk, General

Performs any combination of clerical duties requiring limited knowledge of systems or procedures: Writes, types, or enters information into computer, using keyboard, to prepare correspondence, bills, statements, receipts, cheques, or other documents, copying information from one record to another. Proofreads records or forms. Counts, weighs, or measures material. Sorts and files records. Receives money from customers and deposits money in bank. Addresses envelopes or packages by hand or with machine. Stuffs envelopes by hand or with envelope stuffing machine. Answers telephone, conveys messages, and runs errands. Stamps, sorts, and distributes mail. Stamps or numbers forms by hand or machine. Photocopies documents. GED: R3 M2 L3. SVP: 3.

Clerk, Sales

Obtains or receives merchandise, totals bill, accepts payment, and makes change for customers in retail store such as tobacco shop, drug store, candy store, or liquor store: Stocks shelves, counters, or tables with merchandise. Sets up advertising displays or arranges merchandise on counters or tables to promote sales. Stamps, marks, or tags price on merchandise. Obtains merchandise requested by customer or receives merchandise selected by customer. Answers customers' questions concerning location, price, and use of merchandise. Totals price and tax on merchandise purchased by customer, using paper and pencil, cash register, or calculator to determine bill. Accepts payment and makes change. Wraps or bags merchandise for customers. Cleans shelves, counters, or tables. Removes and records amount of cash in register at end of shift. May calculate sales discount to determine price. May keep record of sales, prepare inventory of stock, or order merchandise. May be designated according to product sold or type of store. GED: R3 M2 L2. SVP: 3.

Computer Programmer

Converts data from project specifications and statements of problems and procedures to create or modify computer programs: Receives from Systems Analyst detailed workflow chart and diagram to illustrate sequence of steps that program must follow and to describe input, output, and logical operations involved. Analyzes workflow chart and diagram, applying knowledge of computer capabilities, subject matter, and symbolic logic. Confers with supervisor to resolve questions of program intent, data input, output requirements, and inclusion of internal checks and controls. Converts detailed logical flow chart to language processable by computer. Enters program codes into computer system. Inputs test data into computer. Observes computer monitor to interpret program operating codes. Corrects program errors. Compiles documentation of program development and subsequent revisions. May train workers to use program. May assist Computer Operator (clerical) to resolve problems in running computer program. May work with Systems Analyst to obtain and analyze project specifications and flow charts. GED: R5 M4 L5. SVP: 5.

Janitor

Keeps hotel, office building, apartment house, or similar building in clean and orderly condition and tends furnace, air-conditioner, and boiler to provide heat, cool air, and hot water for tenants, performing any combination of following duties: Sweeps, mops, scrubs, and vacuums hallways, stairs, and office space. Regulates flow of fuel into automatic furnace or shovels coal into hand-fired furnace. Empties tenants' trash and garbage containers. Maintains building, performing minor and routine painting, plumbing, electrical wiring, and other related maintenance activities, using handtools. Replaces air-conditioner filters. Cautions tenants regarding complaints about excessive noise, disorderly conduct, or misuse of property. Notifies management concerning need for major repairs or additions to lighting, heating, and ventilating equipment. Cleans snow and debris from sidewalk. Mows lawn, trims shrubbery, and cultivates flowers, using handtools and power tools. GED: R3 M2 L3. SVP: 3.

Manager, Department

Directs and coordinates, through subordinate supervisors, department activities in commercial, industrial, or service establishment: Reviews and analyzes reports, records, and directives, and confers with supervisors to obtain data required for planning department activities, such as new commitments, status of work in progress, and problems encountered. Assigns, or delegates responsibility for, specified work or functional activities and disseminates policy to supervisors. Gives work directions, resolves problems, prepares schedules, and sets deadlines to ensure timely completion of work. Coordinates activities of department with related activities of other departments to ensure efficiency and economy. Monitors and analyzes costs and prepares budget, using computer. Prepares reports and records on department activities for management, using computer. Evaluates current procedures and practices for accomplishing department objectives to develop and implement improved procedures and practices. May initiate or authorize employee hire, promotion, discharge, or transfer. Workers are designated according to functions, activities, or type of department managed. GED: R5 M5 L4. SVP: 8.

Manager, Engineering, Electronics

Directs and coordinates activities of engineering department to design, manufacture, and test electronic components, products, and systems: Directs department activities, through subordinates, to design new products, modify existing designs, improve production techniques, and develop test procedures. Analyzes technology trends, human resource needs, and market demand to plan projects. Confers with management, production, and marketing staff to determine engineering feasibility, cost-effectiveness, and customer demand for new and existing products. Forecasts operating costs of department and directs preparation of budget requests. Directs personnel activities of department, such as recruitment, hiring, performance evaluations, and salary adjustments. May direct field testing of products and systems. GED: R6 M6 L5. SVP: 9.

Manager, General

Under the direction of the Chief Executive Officer, directs and coordinates activities of business organization to obtain optimum efficiency and economy of operations: Plans, develops, and implements goals and organization policies through subordinate administrative personnel. Coordinates activities of divisions or departments, such as operating, manufacturing, engineering, planning, sales, maintenance, or research and development, to effect operational efficiency and economy. Directs and coordinates promotion of products manufactured or services performed to develop new markets, increase share of market, and obtain competitive position in industry. Analyzes division or department budget requests to identify areas in which reductions can be made, and allocates operating budget. Confers with administrative personnel, and reviews activity, operating, and sales reports to determine changes in programs or operations required. Directs preparation of directives to division or department administrators outlining policy, program, or operations changes to be implemented. Promotes organization in industry, manufacturing, or trade associations. GED: R6 M5 L5. SVP: 9.

Manager, Office

Coordinates activities of clerical personnel in establishment or organization: Analyzes and organizes office operations and procedures, such as typing, bookkeeping, preparation of payrolls, flow of correspondence, filing, requisition of supplies, and other clerical services. Evaluates office production, revises procedures, or devises new forms to improve efficiency of workflow. Establishes uniform correspondence procedures and style practices. Formulates procedures for systematic retention, protection, retrieval, transfer, and disposal of records. Plans office layouts and initiates cost reduction programs. Reviews clerical and personnel records to ensure completeness, accuracy, and timeliness. Prepares activities reports for guidance of management, using computer. Prepares employee ratings and conducts employee benefit and insurance programs, using computer. Coordinates activities of various clerical departments or workers within department. May prepare organizational budget and monthly financial reports. May hire, train, and supervise clerical staff. GED: R4 M3 L4. SVP: 7.

Manager, Sales

Manages sales activities of establishment: Directs staffing, training, and performance evaluations to develop and control sales program. Coordinates sales distribution by establishing sales territories, quotas, and goals and advises dealers, distributors, and clients concerning sales and advertising techniques. Assigns sales territory to sales personnel. Analyzes sales statistics to formulate policy and to assist dealers in promoting sales. Reviews market analyses to determine customer needs, volume potential, price schedules, and discount rates, and develops sales campaigns to accommodate goals of company. Directs product simplification and standardization to eliminate unprofitable items from sales line. Represents company at trade association meetings to promote product. Coordinates liaison between sales department and other sales-related units. Analyzes and controls expenditures of division to conform to budgetary requirements. Assists other departments within establishment to prepare manuals and technical publications. Prepares periodic sales report showing sales volume and potential sales. May direct sales for manufacturer, retail store, wholesale house, jobber, or other establishment. May direct product research and development. May recommend or approve budget, expenditures, and appropriations for research and development work. GED: R5 M5 L5. SVP: 8.

Personnel Recruiter

Seeks out, interviews, screens, and recruits job applicants to fill existing company job openings: Discusses personnel needs with department supervisors to prepare and implement recruitment program. Contacts colleges to arrange on-campus interviews. Provides information on company facilities and job opportunities to potential applicants. Interviews college applicants to obtain work history, education, training, job skills, and salary requirements. Screens and refers qualified applicants to company hiring personnel for follow-up interview. Arranges travel and lodging for selected applicants at company expense. Performs reference and background checks on applicants. Corresponds with job applicants to notify them of employment consideration. Files and maintains employment records for future references. Projects yearly recruitment expenditures for budgetary control. GED: R5 M3 L5. SVP: 7.

Programmer/Analyst

Plans, develops, tests, and documents computer programs, applying knowledge of programming techniques and computer systems: Evaluates user request for new or modified program, such as for financial or human resource management system, clinical research trial results, statistical study of traffic patterns, or analyzing and developing specifications for bridge design, to determine feasibility, cost and time required, compatibility with current system, and computer capabilities. Reads manuals, periodicals, and technical reports to learn ways to develop programs that meet user requirements. Formulates plan outlining steps required to develop program, using structured analysis and design. Prepares flow charts and diagrams to illustrate sequence of steps program must follow and to describe logical operations involved. Converts project specifications, using flow charts and diagrams, into sequence of detailed instructions and logical steps for coding into language processable by computer, applying knowledge of computer programming techniques and computer languages. Enters program codes into computer system. Enters commands into computer to run and test program. Reads computer printouts or observes display screen to detect syntax or logic errors during program test, or uses diagnostic software to detect errors. Replaces, deletes, or modifies codes to correct errors. Analyzes, reviews, and alters program to increase operating efficiency or adapt to new requirements. Writes documentation to describe program development, logic, coding, and corrections. Writes manual for users to describe installation and operating procedures. May train users to use program. May oversee installation of hardware and software. May provide technical assistance to program users. May install and test program at user site. May monitor performance of program after implementation. May specialize in developing programs for business or technical applications. May direct and coordinate work of others to write, test, and modify computer programs. GED: R5 M5 L5. SVP: 7.

Sales Representative, Commercial Products/Services

Contacts representatives of government, business, and industrial organizations to solicit business for employer: Calls on prospective clients to explain types of products/services provided by establishment, analyzes requirements of prospective client and draws up prospectus of products/services that will meet client's needs. Quotes prices for products/ services outlined in prospectus. Revises or expands prospectus to meet client's needs. Writes order and schedules initiation of services. Periodically confers with clients and establishment personnel to verify satisfaction with service or to resolve complaints. GED: R5 M5 L5. SVP: 7.

Secretary

Schedules appointments, gives information to callers, takes dictation, and otherwise relieves officials of clerical work and minor administrative and business detail: Reads and routes incoming mail. Locates and attaches appropriate file to correspondence to be answered by employer. Transcribes minutes of meetings on word processor or transcribes from voice recordings. Composes and types routine correspondence. Files correspondence and other records. Answers telephone and gives information to callers or routes call to appropriate official and places outgoing calls. Greets visitors, ascertains nature of business, and conducts visitors to appropriate person. May arrange travel schedules and reservations. May compile and type statistical reports. May oversee clerical workers. May record minutes of staff meetings. May make copies of correspondence or other printed matter, using copying machine. May prepare outgoing mail, using postage-metering machine. GED: R4 M3 L4. SVP: 6.

Supervisor, Technical Services, Electrical Machinery

Able to undertake, supervise, and conduct training of technicians in service activities across the full range of a specified product category of electrical machinery. Able to read specifications, such as blueprints, charts, and schematics, to determine machine settings and adjustments. Able to assemble machines according to specifications, using hand tools, power tools, and measuring devices. Able to perform all types of required maintenance and servicing. Able to test machine to locate cause of electrical or mechanical malfunctions. Able to repair, adjust, or replace electrical and mechanical components and parts. Instructs operators, servicers, and technicians in operation, maintenance, and repair of machines. GED: R4 M4 L4. SVP: 8.

Systems Analyst

Analyzes user requirements, procedures, and problems to automate processing or to improve existing computer system: Confers with personnel of organizational units involved to analyze current operational procedures, identify problems, and learn specific input and output requirements, such as forms of data input, how data is to be summarized, and formats for reports. Writes detailed description of user needs, program functions, and steps required to develop or modify computer program. Reviews computer system capabilities, workflow, and scheduling limitations to determine if requested program or program change is possible within existing system. Studies existing information processing systems to evaluate effectiveness and develops new systems to improve production or workflow as required. Prepares workflow charts and diagrams to specify in detail operations to be performed by equipment and computer programs and operations to be performed by personnel in system. Conducts studies pertaining to development of new information systems to meet current and projected needs. Plans and prepares technical reports, memoranda, and instructional manuals as documentation of program development. Upgrades system and corrects errors to maintain system after implementation. May assist Computer Programmer in resolution of work problems related to flow charts, project specifications, or programming. May prepare time and cost estimates for completing projects. May direct and coordinate work of others to develop, test, install, and modify programs. GED: R5 M4 L5. SVP: 7.

Systems Programmer

Coordinates installation of computer operating system software and tests, maintains, and modifies software, using computer terminal: Reads loading and running instructions for system software, such as task scheduling, memory management, computer file system, or controlling computer input and output, and loads tape into tape drive or transfers software to magnetic disk. Initiates test of system program and observes readout on monitor of computer system to detect errors or work stoppage. Enters code changes into computer system to correct errors. Analyzes performance indicators, such as system's response time, number of transactions per second, and number of programs being processed at once, to ensure that system is operating efficiently. Changes system software so that system performance will meet objectives. Reviews computer system capabilities, workflow, and scheduling limitations to determine if requested changes to operating system are possible. Writes description of steps taken to modify system and procedures required to implement new software. Assists users having problems with use of system software. May train users, Computer Operator, and Computer Programmer to use system software. May prepare workflow charts and diagrams to modify system software. May visit vendors to observe demonstration of systems software. May administer and monitor computer program that controls user access to system. May review productivity reports and problem records to evaluate performance of computer system. GED: R5 M4 L5. SVP: 7.

Technical Support Specialist

Performs any combination of the following duties to provide technical support to workers in information processing departments: Develops work goals and department projects. Assigns and coordinates work projects, such as converting to new hardware or software.

Designates staff assignments, establishes work priorities, and evaluates cost and time requirements. Reviews completed projects or computer programs to ensure that goals are met and that programs are compatible with other programs already in use. Evaluates work load and capacity of computer system to determine feasibility of expanding or enhancing computer operations. Makes recommendations for improvements in computer system. Reviews and tests programs written by Programmer/Analyst or Computer Programmer to ensure that programs meet objectives and specifications. Consults with Quality Assurance Analyst to ensure that program follows establishment standards. Modifies, tests, and corrects existing programs. Evaluates and tests vendor-supplied software packages for mainframe computer or microcomputers to determine compatibility with existing system, ease of use, and if software meets user needs. Enters commands into computer to place programs in production status. Tests computer system to determine criticality of component loss. Prioritizes importance of components and writes recommendations for recovering losses and using backup equipment. Assists user to resolve problems such as inoperative hardware or software. Trains workers in use of new software or hardware. Reads technical journals or manuals and attends vendor seminars to learn about new computer hardware and software. Writes documentation for new or modified software and hardware. GED: R5 M4 L5. SVP: 7.

Technician, Apprentice, Electrical Machinery

Under the supervision of senior technician, assembles and installs machine according to specifications, using hand tools, power tools, and measuring devices. Reads specifications, such as blueprints, charts, and schematics to determine machine settings and adjustments. Operates machine to test functioning of parts and mechanisms. Performs routine servicing, by cleaning and oiling mechanical parts, and disassembling machine to examine parts, such as wires, gears, and bearings, for wear and defects. Instructs operators in operation of machine. May perform some activities without direct supervision.
GED: R4 M4 L3. SVP: 6.

Training Officer

Develops and conducts training programs for employees of industrial, commercial, service, or government establishment: Confers with management to gain knowledge of work situation requiring training for employees to better understand changes in policies, procedures, regulations, and technologies. Formulates teaching outline and determines instructional methods, utilizing knowledge of specified training needs and effectiveness of such methods as individual training, group instruction, lectures, demonstrations, conferences, meetings, and workshops. Selects or develops teaching aids, such as training handbooks, demonstration models, multimedia visual aids, computer tutorials, and reference works. Conducts training sessions covering specified areas such as those concerned with new employee orientation, on-the-job training, use of computers and software, apprenticeship programs, sales techniques, health and safety practices, public relations, refresher training, promotional development, upgrading, retraining displaced workers, and leadership development. Tests trainees to measure progress and to evaluate effectiveness of training. May specialize in developing instructional software.
GED: R5 M4 L5. SVP: 7.

CompSoft (Phase II) Screens and Example

Copies of each CompSoft screen in Phase II are shown on the following pages, along with an example illustrating usage of the software. Special notes for some of the screens, explaining an example of software usage, are shown in italics. One good way of learning the software would be to work through this example, inserting data as in the example. *But note that this example illustrates only how to use CompSoft; it does not necessarily result in a good compensation system, or reflect high-quality compensation decisions along the way.*

CompSoft is a Microsoft "Excel"-based spreadsheet program, which uses a "Windows" platform. Your instructor will give you instructions on how to access CompSoft Phase II. A CD is also included with this manual. If you are using the CD as the source of your software, follow the instructions (on page 110) carefully for loading it on your system.

Some final tips. Be sure to do the relevant reading in the text *before* attempting to work your way through CompSoft. CompSoft is not a shortcut to understanding. On its own, CompSoft will not teach you how to design an effective compensation system. Its only purpose is to help you structure your thinking, perform the calculations required for parts of the compensation process, and provide the market data that you need to calibrate your new compensation system.

When CompSoft asks you to do something, be sure that you understand *why* it is doing so before you continue. When CompSoft provides some output, make sure you know what that output means before going on. Finally, remember that there is lot more to Phase II than simply following through CompSoft; there are several important sections that use CompSoft very little or not at all. Moreover, even for the sections that do utilize CompSoft, your explanation of *why* you are handling each step the way you have is just as important as the output from CompSoft.

NAVIGATION

Introduction		
Screen 1	Screen 4	Screen 7
Screen 2	Screen 5	Screen 8
Screen 3	Screen 6	Screen 9

CompSoft Phase II

Compensation Simulation Software (4th Edition 2010)

To accompany Richard J. Long's *Strategic Compensation in Canada* published by Nelson Education, Toronto, 4th Edition, 2010.

Software Development:

H.S. Ravichander, BSc, DBM, AGS (Indiana-Purdue), MBA (Sask)
Sessional Lecturer
Edwards School of Business
University of Saskatchewan
Email: ravichander@edwards.usask.ca

Next   Exit

GENERAL INSTRUCTIONS (COMPATIBLE WITH EXCEL 2003 - 2007)

1) This is the software (CompSoft) for Phase II of the Compensation Simulation Project. Phase I of the project should have been completed before you begin work on Phase II. Strategies developed in Phase I will be used in this phase of the simulation.

2) There are a total of nine screens in Phase II.

3) Follow the instructions provided on each screen. Note that these instructions are primarily related to the use of CompSoft. The instructions do not tell you how to develop an effective compensation system. You must first read the relevant sections of the textbook to gain the compensation knowledge required to work through CompSoft.

4) Click "Save" on each screen where it is available to save your data. When saving your CompSoft file on Excel, DO NOT alter the name of the file in any way! This can cause unpredictable consequences.

5) If you wish to print any of the screens for review and decisionmaking, you may do so using Excel's own menus for printing. Before printing, highlight the area you wish to print, and click "Selection" on Excel's print control screen.

6) The "Next" and "Return" buttons on the screens are merely for navigation purposes and as such do not process any data.

7) The "Retrieve" buttons on the following screens restore data that you have previously entered and saved.

8) Before printing a graph, click on the graph and then use Excel's print command.

DO NOT ATTEMPT TO MOVE, CUT, PASTE, EDIT, RE-ENGINEER OR REVERSE ENGINEER ANY OF THE PROGRAMMED OBJECTS AND CODE IN THIS SOFTWARE. NON-COMPLIANCE COULD LEAD TO UNPREDICTABLE RESULTS AND IS IN VIOLATION OF THE AUTHOR'S WORK.

| Next | Return |

PHASE II - SCREEN 1

1) Below is a list of 24 companies for which compensation survey information has been collected.

2) Your objective here is to select the companies to use as sources of market data for your client firm.

3) This is accomplished by entering a "y" for each row in the column titled "Include?". Press the ENTER key to confirm each entry.

4) Click "Save" to save your entries. (If you have previously completed this step, click "Retrieve" to obtain this previous data.)

5) Click "Display Data" to display the data for the companies chosen.

6) You must always click "Display Data" before proceeding to the next screen.

Save   Retrieve   Display Data   Return   Clear Selection

Company Number	Company Name	Industry	Product Line	# Of Emps.	Main Base of Operations	Include?	
1	Atlantic Telecom	Communications	Telecommunications	8,000	Atlantic Canada	y	Selected
2	Bank of New Brunswick	Financial Services	Financial Services	20,000	National	y	Selected
3	BGC Data Services	Business Services	Data Processing	1,700	National	y	Selected
4	Business Supply Depot	Retail	Business Products	3,000	National	y	Selected
5	Can Pharm Ltd	Manufacturing	Pharmaceuticals	1,450	Quebec	y	Selected
6	Central Business Mach.	Sales/Service	Office Machines	650	Ontario/Quebec		
7	EAB Electronics	Manufacturing	Electronic Products	4,200	Ontario		
8	Forhealth Ltd	Manufacturing	Pharmaceuticals	687	Quebec		
9	Kanon Corporation	Retail/Wholesale	Cameras/Copiers	1,300	National		
10	Lanfield Industries	Manufacturing	Aerospace Compon.	321	Ontario		
11	Lorax Entertainment	Cultural/Recreational	Television Programs	2,600	Ontario		
12	Net-Space Communic.	Communications	Cellular Communic.	2,500	Atlantic Canada		
13	Pacific Telecom	Communications	Telecommunications	15,000	Western Canada		
14	PPI Industries	Manufacturing	Pumps & Valves	800	Ontario		
15	Purple Cross Insurance	Health Services	Health Insurance	1,147	Quebec		
16	Scandia Furniture Ltd	Retail	Furniture	500	Ontario		
17	Scott MacDonald Group	Business Services	Consumer Research	1,000	Ontario		
18	Smithers Data Services	Business Services	Data Processing	1,000	National		
19	Space-Dev Inc	Manufacturing	Satellite Navigation Sys	830	Ontario		
20	Terran Oil	Resources	Petroleum Products	6,500	Western Canada		
21	Western Office Mach.	Sales/Service	Office Machines	350	Western Canada		
22	Zebra Electronics	Manufacturing	Electronic Products	1,100	Ontario		
23	Zorgwell Controls	Manufacturing	Electronic Products	5,600	Ontario		
24	Zorel Software Corp.	Computer Products	Computer Software	1,600	Ontario		

PHASE II - SCREEN 2

1) In this screen, your objective is to select the market comparator jobs that match your benchmark jobs, to calibrate your job evaluation system.
2) You MUST SELECT A MINIMUM OF 3 UNIQUE JOBS (preferably more).
3) For each market comparator job you choose, enter a "y" in the "Include Job?" column for ALL the listings for that job title. Press ENTER or the UP/DOWN ARROWS on your keyboard to move down the list.
4) Click "Clear Selection" if you wish to delete your entries. Click "Save" to store your selection.
5) Once you have made your selections, click "Display Comparator Jobs" to display data for the comparator jobs.

| Save | Retrieve | Display Comparator Jobs | Return | Clear Selection |

CompSoft Example Screen 2

Screen 2 displays all the compensation data for each of the market comparator firms that you selected in Screen 1. We have selected "Accountant, Tax," "Janitor," "Manager, Department," "Manager, Office," and "Secretary" as market comparator jobs to match our "Accountant," "Caretaker," "Director of Human Resources," "Compensation Manager," and "Secretary" benchmark jobs. Note that these may or may not be good choices. Be sure to type "y" for all the firms that have market comparator jobs that match your benchmark jobs. (This screen is continued on the next page.)

Company Number	Company Name	Job Title	Emps. In Job	Base Pay Range Minimum	Maximum	Mean Base Pay	Individual Performance Pay	Group/Org. Performance Pay	Indirect Pay	Mean Total Compensation	Include Job?
1	Atlantic Telecom	Accountant, Tax	4	$52,800	$70,400	$61,600	$1,100	$3,300	$8,800	$74,800	y
2	Bank of New Brunswick	Accountant, Tax	13	$60,500	$78,100	$71,500	$2,200	$2,750	$13,750	$90,200	y
3	BGC Data Services	Accountant, Tax	1	$62,700	$80,300	$73,700	$1,650	$0	$12,100	$87,450	y
4	Business Supply Depot	Accountant, Tax	3	$51,700	$68,200	$61,600	$0	$2,750	$8,800	$73,150	y
5	Can Pharm Ltd	Accountant, Tax	1	$60,500	$84,700	$71,500	$2,750	$1,760	$14,300	$90,310	y
1	Atlantic Telecom	Clerk, Accounting	8	$27,500	$37,400	$31,900	$0	$1,100	$6,600	$39,600	
2	Bank of New Brunswick	Clerk, Accounting	26	$30,800	$41,800	$36,300	$0	$1,320	$8,250	$45,870	
3	BGC Data Services	Clerk, Accounting	2	$34,100	$42,900	$39,600	$0	$0	$8,800	$48,400	
4	Business Supply Depot	Clerk, Accounting	10	$30,250	$36,850	$33,550	$0	$1,320	$6,600	$41,470	
5	Can Pharm Ltd	Clerk, Accounting	2	$33,000	$42,900	$37,400	$0	$880	$9,350	$47,630	
1	Atlantic Telecom	Clerk, Administrative	16	$24,860	$34,650	$29,700	$0	$990	$6,270	$36,960	
2	Bank of New Brunswick	Clerk, Administrative	50	$29,260	$38,610	$34,100	$0	$1,210	$7,920	$43,230	
3	BGC Data Services	Clerk, Administrative	8	$31,900	$40,700	$37,400	$0	$0	$8,470	$45,870	
4	Business Supply Depot	Clerk, Administrative	60	$29,150	$35,750	$32,450	$0	$1,100	$6,380	$39,930	
5	Can Pharm Ltd	Clerk, Administrative	4	$30,800	$40,700	$35,200	$0	$770	$9,130	$45,100	
1	Atlantic Telecom	Clerk, General	32	$20,900	$30,800	$25,300	$0	$770	$5,940	$32,010	
2	Bank of New Brunswick	Clerk, General	100	$24,200	$34,100	$28,600	$0	$880	$7,480	$36,960	
3	BGC Data Services	Clerk, General	8	$27,500	$37,400	$31,900	$0	$0	$7,700	$39,600	
4	Business Supply Depot	Clerk, General	24	$23,100	$30,800	$27,500	$0	$880	$5,500	$33,880	
5	Can Pharm Ltd	Clerk, General	4	$25,300	$35,200	$29,700	$0	$550	$8,580	$38,830	
1	Atlantic Telecom	Clerk, Sales	100	$13,042	$19,558	$16,764	$990	$990	$3,366	$22,110	
4	Business Supply Depot	Clerk, Sales	1500	$19,880	$24,200	$23,100	$5,500	$880	$5,500	$34,980	
1	Atlantic Telecom	Computer Prog.	100	$37,180	$50,490	$42,350	$550	$1,650	$7,480	$52,030	
2	Bank of New Brunswick	Computer Prog.	50	$40,920	$54,175	$46,585	$1,320	$1,980	$9,900	$59,785	
3	BGC Data Services	Computer Prog.	20	$44,110	$57,750	$50,160	$1,100	$0	$9,900	$61,160	
4	Business Supply Depot	Computer Prog.	8	$41,800	$49,500	$47,300	$0	$2,200	$7,700	$57,200	
5	Car Pharm Ltd	Computer Prog.	6	$43,010	$56,430	$48,510	$1,650	$1,320	$10,450	$61,930	
1	Atlantic Telecom	Janitor	16	$20,898	$25,958	$23,327	$0	$708	$5,465	$29,500	y
2	Bank of New Brunswick	Janitor	100	$23,664	$29,172	$26,418	$0	$816	$6,936	$34,170	y
3	BGC Data Services	Janitor	8	$27,223	$32,384	$29,550	$0	$0	$7,084	$36,634	y
4	Business Supply Depot	Janitor	60	$22,264	$26,312	$24,288	$0	$708	$5,060	$30,056	y
5	Can Pharm Ltd	Janitor	5	$25,401	$30,664	$27,830	$0	$506	$7,894	$36,230	y

#	Company	Position	Count								
1	Atlantic Telecom	Manager, Dept.	10	$55,275	$68,200	$60,445	$6,820	$4,730	$9,460	$81,455	y
2	Bank of New Brunswick	Manager, Dept.	25	$62,150	$81,400	$69,300	$8,800	$7,700	$14,300	$100,100	y
3	BGC Data Services	Manager, Dept.	9	$70,400	$90,200	$78,100	$12,650	$0	$14,300	$105,050	y
4	Business Supply Depot	Manager, Dept.	8	$60,500	$82,500	$71,500	$5,500	$5,500	$12,100	$94,600	y
5	Can Pharm Ltd	Manager, Dept.	6	$64,900	$88,000	$72,600	$11,550	$8,800	$15,400	$108,350	y
2	Bank of New Brunswick	Manager, General	1	$203,500	$247,500	$225,500	$0	$115,500	$41,800	$382,800	
3	BGC Data Services	Manager, General	1	$266,200	$310,200	$288,200	$0	$143,000	$51,700	$482,900	
4	Business Supply Depot	Manager, General	1	$145,200	$189,200	$167,200	$0	$88,000	$30,800	$286,000	
5	Can Pharm Ltd	Manager, General	1	$231,000	$275,000	$253,000	$0	$126,500	$47,300	$426,800	
1	Atlantic Telecom	Manager, Office	20	$33,110	$45,320	$40,480	$440	$1,430	$7,150	$49,500	y
2	Bank of New Brunswick	Manager, Office	200	$35,640	$47,850	$43,560	$1,100	$1,760	$9,020	$55,440	y
3	BGC Data Services	Manager, Office	20	$40,150	$52,250	$46,750	$880	$0	$9,350	$56,980	y
4	Business Supply Depot	Manager, Office	10	$37,400	$44,000	$40,700	$0	$1,760	$7,150	$49,610	y
5	Can Pharm Ltd	Manager, Office	9	$37,950	$50,050	$44,550	$1,430	$1,210	$9,900	$57,090	y
1	Atlantic Telecom	Manager, Sales	1	$91,080	$121,440	$97,405	$18,034	$24,824	$23,934	$164,197	
2	Bank of New Brunswick	Manager, Sales	1	$101,200	$131,560	$119,112	$20,372	$29,834	$29,055	$198,372	
3	BGC Data Services	Manager, Sales	1	$101,200	$131,560	$116,127	$19,785	$28,387	$27,957	$192,255	
4	Business Supply Depot	Manager, Sales	1	$111,200	$141,680	$121,440	$30,360	$30,360	$25,300	$207,460	
5	Can Pharm Ltd	Manager, Sales	1	$111,320	$123,464	$117,392	$20,240	$28,741	$28,336	$194,709	
1	Atlantic Telecom	Personnel Recruiter	12	$39,050	$52,800	$44,000	$605	$1,760	$7,700	$54,065	
2	Bank of New Brunswick	Personnel Recruiter	40	$41,800	$53,900	$47,850	$1,430	$2,090	$10,120	$61,490	
3	BGC Data Services	Personnel Recruiter	3	$46,200	$59,400	$52,800	$1,320	$0	$10,230	$64,350	
4	Business Supply Depot	Personnel Recruiter	6	$39,600	$46,200	$42,900	$0	$1,980	$7,480	$52,360	
5	Can Pharm Ltd	Personnel Recruiter	3	$44,000	$55,000	$49,500	$1,760	$1,430	$10,560	$63,250	
1	Atlantic Telecom	Programmer/Analyst	10	$55,000	$71,500	$62,260	$1,155	$3,410	$8,910	$75,735	
2	Bank of New Brunswick	Programmer/Analyst	10	$59,400	$78,100	$69,300	$1,980	$2,530	$13,200	$87,010	
3	BGC Data Services	Programmer/Analyst	4	$62,700	$78,100	$71,940	$1,595	$0	$11,880	$85,415	
4	Business Supply Depot	Programmer/Analyst	8	$60,500	$71,500	$66,000	$0	$3,080	$9,350	$78,430	
5	Can Pharm Ltd	Programmer/Analyst	2	$60,500	$79,200	$69,300	$2,530	$1,705	$13,860	$87,395	
1	Atlantic Telecom	Sales Rep.	100	$28,600	$39,600	$34,100	$13,200	$1,980	$7,370	$56,650	
3	BGC Data Services	Sales Rep.	25	$38,500	$49,500	$44,000	$16,500	$1,980	$10,780	$71,280	
4	Business Supply Depot	Sales Rep.	150	$28,600	$37,400	$33,000	$13,200	$2,200	$8,250	$56,650	
5	Can Pharm Ltd	Sales Rep.	150	$35,200	$48,400	$41,800	$16,500	$1,650	$11,000	$70,950	
1	Atlantic Telecom	Secretary	20	$30,250	$42,350	$35,750	$0	$1,210	$6,930	$43,890	y
2	Bank of New Brunswick	Secretary	50	$34,100	$46,200	$39,050	$0	$1,485	$8,525	$49,060	y
3	BGC Data Services	Secretary	20	$37,400	$49,500	$42,680	$0	$0	$9,185	$51,865	y
4	Business Supply Depot	Secretary	30	$34,100	$41,800	$38,500	$0	$1,650	$6,930	$47,080	y
5	Can Pharm Ltd	Secretary	15	$34,650	$46,750	$40,150	$550	$1,018	$9,625	$50,793	y
1	Atlantic Telecom	Supervisor, Tech Serv	100	$38,110	$51,753	$43,409	$550	$1,692	$7,667	$53,318	
4	Business Supply Depot	Supervisor, Tech Serv	15	$40,700	$52,800	$47,300	$0	$2,200	$7,700	$57,200	
1	Atlantic Telecom	Systems Analyst	5	$49,500	$61,600	$55,990	$880	$2,750	$7,920	$67,540	
2	Bank of New Brunswick	Systems Analyst	10	$51,700	$65,450	$58,300	$1,650	$2,310	$11,550	$73,810	
1	Atlantic Telecom	Systems Prog.	5	$49,500	$61,600	$55,550	$880	$2,750	$7,920	$67,100	
2	Bank of New Brunswick	Systems Prog.	15	$52,250	$66,000	$58,850	$1,650	$2,310	$11,550	$74,360	
5	Can Pharm Ltd	Systems Prog.	1	$53,350	$67,650	$59,400	$2,200	$1,540	$12,320	$75,460	
1	Atlantic Telecom	Tech Support Spec.	20	$49,500	$61,600	$56,100	$880	$2,750	$7,920	$67,650	
2	Bank of New Brunswick	Tech Support Spec.	30	$52,250	$66,000	$59,400	$1,650	$2,310	$11,550	$74,910	
3	BGC Data Services	Tech Support Spec.	10	$56,100	$69,850	$62,150	$1,375	$0	$11,000	$74,525	
4	Business Supply Depot	Tech Support Spec.	5	$51,700	$62,700	$57,200	$0	$2,530	$8,580	$68,310	
5	Can Pharm Ltd	Tech Support Spec.	5	$53,350	$67,650	$58,850	$2,200	$1,540	$12,320	$74,910	
1	Atlantic Telecom	Tech, App, Elec.	250	$21,670	$23,870	$22,770	$550	$693	$5,346	$28,809	
4	Business Supply Depot	Tech, App, Elec.	30	$23,100	$25,300	$24,200	$0	$550	$4,950	$29,700	
1	Atlantic Telecom	Training Officer	25	$33,000	$50,600	$44,000	$605	$1,815	$7,590	$54,010	
2	Bank of New Brunswick	Training Officer	25	$36,300	$51,700	$47,300	$1,375	$2,063	$10,120	$60,858	
3	BGC Data Services	Training Officer	3	$41,800	$53,900	$51,700	$1,155	$0	$10,120	$62,975	
4	Business Supply Depot	Training Officer	4	$40,700	$47,300	$45,100	$0	$2,090	$7,590	$54,780	
5	Can Pharm Ltd	Training Officer	2	$38,500	$53,350	$49,500	$1,705	$1,375	$10,780	$63,360	

PHASE II - SCREEN 3

1) This table contains the relevant data for the market comparator jobs you chose in the previous screen.
2) If you wish, print this screen as you normally would in Excel.
3) If satisfied with your results, click "Display Averages and Weighted Averages" or if you wish to revise your choices, click "Return" and make new choices.

| Display Averages and Weighted Averages | Return |

Company Number	Company Name	Job Title	Emps. In Job	Base Pay Range Minimum	Base Pay Range Maximum	Mean Base Pay	Individual Performance Pay	Group/Org. Performance Pay	Indirect Pay	Mean Total Compensation
1	Atlantic Telecom	Accountant, Tax	4	$52,800	$70,400	$61,600	$1,100	$3,300	$8,800	$74,800
2	Bank of New Brunswick	Accountant, Tax	13	$60,500	$78,100	$71,500	$2,200	$2,750	$13,750	$90,200
3	BGC Data Services	Accountant, Tax	1	$62,700	$80,300	$73,700	$1,650	$0	$12,100	$87,450
4	Business Supply Depot	Accountant, Tax	3	$51,700	$68,200	$61,600	$0	$2,750	$8,800	$73,150
5	Can Pharm Ltd	Accountant, Tax	1	$60,500	$84,700	$71,500	$2,750	$1,760	$14,300	$90,310
1	Atlantic Telecom	Janitor	16	$20,898	$25,958	$23,327	$0	$708	$5,465	$29,500
2	Bank of New Brunswick	Janitor	100	$23,664	$29,172	$26,418	$0	$816	$6,936	$34,170
3	BGC Data Services	Janitor	8	$27,223	$32,384	$29,550	$0	$0	$7,084	$36,634
4	Business Supply Depot	Janitor	60	$22,264	$26,312	$24,288	$0	$708	$5,060	$30,056
5	Can Pharm Ltd	Janitor	5	$25,401	$30,664	$27,830	$0	$506	$7,894	$36,230
1	Atlantic Telecom	Manager, Dept.	10	$55,275	$68,200	$60,445	$6,820	$4,730	$9,460	$81,455
2	Bank of New Brunswick	Manager, Dept.	25	$62,150	$81,400	$69,300	$8,800	$7,700	$14,300	$100,100
3	BGC Data Services	Manager, Dept.	9	$70,400	$90,200	$78,100	$12,650	$0	$14,300	$105,050
4	Business Supply Depot	Manager, Dept.	8	$60,500	$82,500	$71,500	$5,500	$5,500	$12,100	$94,600
5	Can Pharm Ltd	Manager, Dept.	6	$64,900	$88,000	$72,600	$11,550	$8,800	$15,400	$108,350
1	Atlantic Telecom	Manager, Office	20	$33,110	$45,320	$40,480	$440	$1,430	$7,150	$49,500
2	Bank of New Brunswick	Manager, Office	200	$35,640	$47,850	$43,560	$1,100	$1,760	$9,020	$55,440
3	BGC Data Services	Manager, Office	20	$40,150	$52,250	$46,750	$880	$0	$9,350	$56,980
4	Business Supply Depot	Manager, Office	10	$37,400	$44,000	$40,700	$0	$1,760	$7,150	$49,610
5	Can Pharm Ltd	Manager, Office	9	$37,950	$50,050	$44,550	$1,430	$1,210	$9,900	$57,090
1	Atlantic Telecom	Secretary	20	$30,250	$42,350	$35,750	$0	$1,210	$6,930	$43,890
2	Bank of New Brunswick	Secretary	50	$34,100	$46,200	$39,050	$0	$1,485	$8,525	$49,060
3	BGC Data Services	Secretary	20	$37,400	$49,500	$42,680	$0	$0	$9,185	$51,865
4	Business Supply Depot	Secretary	30	$34,100	$41,800	$38,500	$0	$1,650	$6,930	$47,080
5	Can Pharm Ltd	Secretary	15	$34,650	$46,750	$40,150	$0	$1,018	$9,625	$50,793

PHASE II - SCREEN 4

1) This screen displays the averages and weighted averages for the market comparator jobs that you selected in the previous screens.

2) If you wish, print this screen as you normally would in Excel.

3) If satisfied with your results, proceed to the next step by clicking "Enter JE Points".

Return		Enter JE Points

Job Title	Emps. In Job	Average Mean Base Pay	Wtd. Avg. Mean Base Pay	Average Mean Ind. Perf. Pay	Wtd. Avg. Mean Ind. Perf. Pay	Average Mean Group/Org. Perf. Pay	Wtd. Avg. Mean Group/Org. Perf. Pay	Average Mean Indirect Pay	Wtd. Avg. Mean Indirect Pay	Average Mean Total Comp.	Weighted Avg. Mean Total Comp.
Accountant, Tax	22	$67,980	$68,450	$1,540	$1,700	$2,112	$2,680	$11,550	$12,125	$83,182	$84,955
Janitor	189	$26,283	$25,650	$0	$0	$548	$730	$6,488	$6,247	$33,318	$32,628
Manager, Dept.	58	$70,389	$69,784	$9,064	$8,885	$5,346	$5,803	$13,112	$13,276	$97,911	$97,748
Manager, Office	259	$43,208	$43,492	$770	$1,001	$1,232	$1,579	$8,514	$8,859	$53,724	$54,932
Secretary	135	$39,226	$39,099	$0	$0	$1,073	$1,209	$8,239	$8,154	$48,538	$48,462

CompSoft Example Screen 4

This screen shows the averages and the weighted averages of the mean base pay, mean individual performance pay, mean group/organizational performance pay, mean indirect pay, and mean total compensation of your market comparators for your benchmark jobs.

- 76 -

INSTRUCTIONS FOR PHASE II - SCREEN 5 (PRINT THESE INSTRUCTIONS)

1) Your objective in Screen 5 is to develop a "Market Line" to calibrate your job evaluation system.

2) Enter the Job Evaluation Points for each of your benchmark jobs. (This information comes from Phase I of your project.)

3) Then, click "Save" to save your data.

4) Click on any ONE of the four measures to produce the market line. Normally, you should use one of the "total compensation" measures.

5) Click "Display Graph". If you wish, print the graph as you would in Excel.

6) After printing the graph, CLICK ON THE BLUE ARROW ON THE SHEET CONTAINING THE GRAPH. You will be returned to Screen 5.

7) Examine your graph carefully, look at the R^2 value; the slope; where your market line would intercept the "y" axis (the b value will tell you this); and the distance of each plot from the market line. Consider what it tells you about whether your job evaluation system is satisfactory as it stands, or whether it needs improvement. (Check your textbook for guidance on this.)

8) If you are satisfied with your results, click "Develop Pay Policy".

PHASE II - SCREEN 5

CLICK ME FOR INSTRUCTIONS BEFORE PROCEEDING WITH ANY
ACTIVITY ON THIS SCREEN

MEASURES

Save	Retrieve	Average Mean Base Pay	Weighted Avg. Mean Base Pay	Display Graph
Return	Reset Measures	Avg. Mean Total Compensation	Wtd. Avg. Mean Total Compensation	Develop Pay Policy

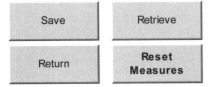

Job Title		Enter JE Points
Accountant, Tax		400
Janitor		150
Manager, Dept.		900
Manager, Office		450
Secretary		250

CompSoft Example
Screen 5

In Phase I, you produced a job evaluation point score for every job in your job evaluation pay structure. Enter the JE point score for your benchmark jobs in the row that corresponds to its matching market comparator job. In this example, "Accountant" received 400 JE points, "Caretaker" received 150 JE points, "Director of Human Resources" received 900 points, "Compensation Manager" received 450 points, and "Secretary" received 250 points, and these have been entered in the rows for the matching market comparator jobs.

After entering the JE points, it is necessary to select one of the four "MEASURES" for the upcoming calculations. We selected the "Weighted Average Mean Total Compensation" but you could have selected "Average Mean Total Compensation." (Do not select either of the other two measures.) In your report, you must explain why you made the choice you did.

Clicking on one of the "MEASURES" and then clicking on the "Display Graph" produces the market line graph shown on the next page.

CompSoft Example
Screen 5
Market Line Graph

Each plot represents a market comparator/bench mark job match. You can tell which plot represents which job by looking at the job evaluation points for each plot. For example, the plot at 150 points represents the janitor/ caretaker match. Examine your graph using concepts from the "Testing for Market Fit" section of Chapter 8. As for the graph shown here, it is not acceptable because of a poor regression coefficient and because there are some strange outliers. For example, the job to which we have allocated 450 JE points is actually valued much lower by the market than the job to which we have allocated 400 points. These things tell us that there may be a problem with our bench mark/ comparator job matches, with our market sample, or with our job evaluation system. In this case, it is probably all three, and must be fixed before you can carry on from here. In this example, we will do what you should not do, and carry on anyway!

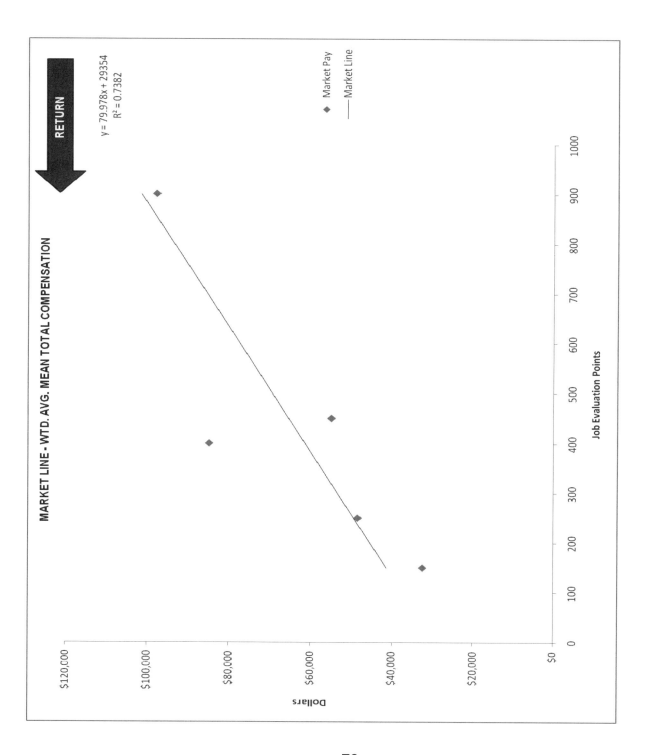

MARKET LINE - WTD. AVG. MEAN TOTAL COMPENSATION

RETURN

y = 79.978x + 29354
R² = 0.7382

◆ Market Pay
—— Market Line

Job Evaluation Points

Dollars

- 79 -

INSTRUCTIONS FOR PHASE II - SCREEN 6 (PRINT THESE INSTRUCTIONS)

1) Your objective in Screen 6 is to create a "Pay Policy Line" for your client firm by incorporating your
   compensation level strategy.
2) If you have the SAME "Lead" or "Lag" policy for ALL jobs in your job evaluation pay structure, enter a "y"
   in the "Lead" or "Lag" decision column, and the percentage "Above" or "Below" the market, according to
   your compensation strategy from Phase I of your project.
3) If you have DIFFERENT "Lead" or "Lag" policies for ANY of the jobs in your job evaluation pay structure,
   OR if you decided to "Match" the market, enter a "y" in the "Match" decision, and leave the percentage field blank.
4) Click "Save" to save your data. Then click on the measure available to generate the
   Pay Policy Graph.
5) Next, click "Display Pay Policy Graph".   Then, print the graph as you would using Excel's menus.
   Write down the values for "mx" and "b" when you view the graph. Be sure to include the minus
   sign (if there is one) for the "b" term.
6) Click on "Develop Pay Structure" to go to the next screen.

PHASE II - SCREEN 6

PAY LEVEL POLICY		
Pay Policy	Decision	Pct.
Lead		
Match		
Lag		

CLICK ME FOR INSTRUCTIONS BEFORE PROCEEDING WITH ANY
ACTIVITY ON THIS SCREEN

MEASURES

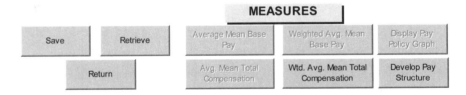

Save	Retrieve	Average Mean Base Pay	Weighted Avg. Mean Base Pay	Display Pay Policy Graph
	Return	Avg. Mean Total Compensation	Wtd. Avg. Mean Total Compensation	Develop Pay Structure

Job Title	Average Mean Base Pay	Weighted Average Mean Base Pay	Average Mean Total Compensation	Weighted Avg. Mean Total Compensation
Accountant, Tax	FALSE	FALSE	FALSE	FALSE
Janitor	FALSE	FALSE	FALSE	FALSE
Manager, Dept.	FALSE	FALSE	FALSE	FALSE
Manager, Office	FALSE	FALSE	FALSE	FALSE
Secretary	FALSE	FALSE	FALSE	FALSE
	FALSE	FALSE	FALSE	FALSE

PHASE II - SCREEN 6

CLICK ME FOR INSTRUCTIONS BEFORE PROCEEDING WITH ANY
ACTIVITY ON THIS SCREEN

PAY LEVEL POLICY

Pay Policy	Decision	Pct.
Lead		
Match	y	
Lag		

MEASURES

Save	Retrieve	Average Mean Base Pay	Weighted Avg. Mean Base Pay	Display Pay Policy Graph
	Return	Avg. Mean Total Compensation	Wtd. Avg. Mean Total Compensation	Develop Pay Structure

Job Title	Average Mean Base Pay	Weighted Average Mean Base Pay	Average Mean Total Compensation	Weighted Avg. Mean Total Compensation
Accountant, Tax	$67,980	$68,450	$83,182	$84,955
Janitor	$26,283	$25,650	$33,318	$32,628
Manager, Dept.	$70,389	$69,784	$97,911	$97,748
Manager, Office	$43,208	$43,492	$53,724	$54,932
Secretary	$39,226	$39,099	$48,538	$48,462

CompSoft Example
Screen 6

At this point, the first thing you need to do is to check your compensation strategy templates from Phase I. Are your compensation level policies the same across all job families? They would be the same if you are, say, planning to <u>lead</u> all jobs by 6%, or if you are planning to <u>lag</u> all jobs by, say, 8%, or if you are planning to match the market for all jobs. If you are planning to lead all jobs by 6%, enter a "y" in the "decision" column in the "pay level policy" box in the "lead" row, and also enter "6" under "pct". If you are planning to lag all jobs by 8%, enter a "y" in the "decision" column in the "pay level policy" box in the "lag" row, and also enter "8" under "pct". If you are planning to match all jobs to the market, just enter a "y" in the "decision" column in the "pay level policy" box in the "match" row.

But what if you are using different compensation level policies for different job families? For example, suppose that you are planning to lead your "management" job family by 5%, lag your "support staff" family by 5%, and match your "professional" job family? In this case, just enter a "y" in the "match" row, and you will make these adjustments later on, in Screen 8. Let us assume that this differential compensation level strategy is our policy, so we have entered a "y" in the "match" row.

Next, we will click on the "MEASURE" that we previously selected ("Weighted Average Mean Total Compensation"), and then on the "Display Pay Policy Graph" button, to produce the pay policy graph that appears on the next page.

- 81 -

CompSoft Example
Screen 6
Pay Policy Graph

If you had selected a "lead" or "lag" strategy in Screen 6, you would see two lines on this graph, with the solid line being your market line, and the broken line being your pay policy line. Your pay policy line would be either above or below your market line, depending on whether you selected a "lead" or a "lag" strategy.

In this case, we selected "match" because we have a differential compensation level strategy, and we will be making our adjustment for that in Screen 8. Therefore our pay policy line is exactly the same as our market line at this point. This will also be true if you selected a "match" strategy because that is your strategy, only you will not have to make any adjustments on Screen 8.

At this point, you should write down the values from your y = mx + b equation above, which are 79.978 (m) and 29,354 (b). In this case, the "b" value has a plus (+) sign in front of it, but it could have a minus (-) sign. If it does, be sure to record the minus sign as well.

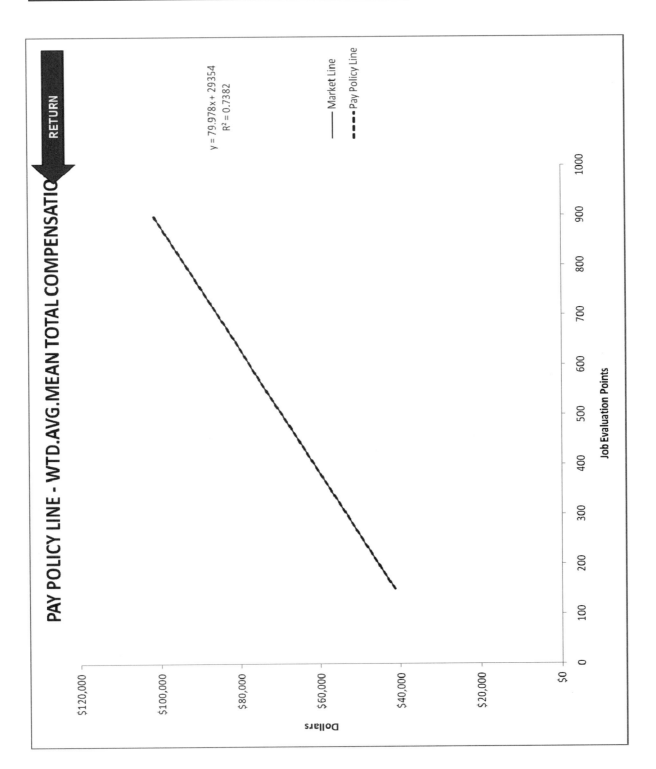

PAY POLICY LINE - WTD.AVG.MEAN TOTAL COMPENSATIO   RETURN

y = 79.978x + 29354
R² = 0.7382

—— Market Line
----- Pay Policy Line

Job Evaluation Points

Dollars

- 82 -

INSTRUCTIONS FOR PHASE II - SCREEN 7 (PRINT THESE INSTRUCTIONS)

1) Your objective in Screen 7 is to create pay grades and pay ranges for the jobs covered by your job evaluation pay structure.

2) Enter the values for the formula $y = mx + b$ (or $mx - b$), that you wrote down from the Pay Policy Graph in Screen 6.

3) Enter the minimum number of job evaluation points *possible* in your job evaluation system.

4) Enter the maximum number of job evaluation points *possible* in your job evaluation system.

5) Enter the number of pay grades that you wish to have in your pay structure.

6) Next, in the table, enter the maximum number of job evaluation points you wish for each pay grade. (CompSoft will automatically enter the minimum JE points for each pay grade.)

7) Next, decide on the minimum dollar value and the maximum dollar value for each pay grade, and enter these values in the "Minimum Dollars" and "Maximum Dollars" columns.

8) Click "Save" to save your data, and then click "Display Pay Structure Graph" to view your pay structure graph.

9) Print this graph as you would in Excel. Click "Return" to go back to Screen 7.

10) Reflect on your JE Pay Structure, and decide whether you are satisfied with it. If not, go back and make the appropriate modifications to your pay grades and pay ranges.

11) If you are satisfied with your JE Pay Structure, click "Next".

PHASE II - SCREEN 7

CLICK ME FOR INSTRUCTIONS BEFORE PROCEEDING WITH ANY ACTIVITY ON THIS SCREEN

Save	Retrieve		Display Pay Structure Graph
	Return		Next

Enter the values for the formula y=mx+b (or mx - b) from the Pay Policy Line Graph

mx=　　　　　　b=

Number of Pay Grades:

Minimum possible JE Points:　　　　　　Maximum possible JE Points:

Pay Grade	Minimum JE Points	Midpoint JE Points	Maximum JE Points	Actual Midpoint Dollars	Minimum Dollars	Maximum Dollars

Save	Retrieve		Display Pay Structure Graph
Return			Next

Enter the values for the formula y=mx+b (or mx - b) from the Pay Policy Line Graph

mx= [79.978]   b= [29354]

Number of Pay Grades: [5]

Minimum possible JE Points: [100]   *Maximum possible JE Points:* [1100]

Pay Grade	Minimum JE Points	Midpoint JE Points	Maximum JE Points	Actual Midpoint Dollars	Minimum Dollars	Maximum Dollars
1	100	50				
2	1	0.5				
3	1	0.5				
4	1	0.5				
5	1	0.5				

CompSoft Example
Screen 7

Based on the equation for our pay policy line produced by Screen 6 (y = 79.978x + 29354), we have entered 79.978 in the "mx" box, and 29354 in the "b" box. We then entered the minimum number of JE points that it is possible for a job to receive under our job evaluation system (the point score if a job had received the lowest possible points for every factor) and the maximum number of JE points that it is possible for a job to receive (the point score if a job had received the highest number of points for every factor). You will get this from your job evaluation system you developed in Phase I. In our example, our minimum possible JE points is 100 and the maximum possible is 1100 (this does not necessarily mean that any job actually received either of these). We entered these in the boxes above.

Next, we have to decide how many pay grades to use. You use your judgment to decide this, based on a few general considerations discussed in Chapter 8. We decided on five grades, entered "5" in the box, and then clicked out of the box. (Note that five grades is not necessarily the correct number. In fact, it is too few for your client!)

PHASE II - SCREEN 7

CLICK ME FOR INSTRUCTIONS BEFORE PROCEEDING WITH ANY
ACTIVITY ON THIS SCREEN

Save	Retrieve		Display Pay Structure Graph
	Return		Next

Enter the values for the formula y=mx+b (or mx - b) from the Pay Policy Line Graph

mx= 79.978   b= 29354

Number of Pay Grades: 5

Minimum possible JE Points: 100   *Maximum possible JE Points:* 1100

Pay Grade	Minimum JE Points	Midpoint JE Points	Maximum JE Points	Actual Midpoint Dollars	Minimum Dollars	Maximum Dollars
1	100	200	300	$45,350		
2	301	400.5	500	$61,385		
3	501	600.5	700	$77,381		
4	701	800.5	900	$93,376		
5	901	1000.5	1100	$109,372		

CompSoft Example
Screen 7

Next, we need to decide the pay grade sizes. Chapter 8 provides guidance on various methods for doing this. In our example, we used the "equal interval" approach, and simply divided the difference between our maximum possible JE points (1100) and our minimum possible JE points (100) by the number of pay grades (5). This results in a pay grade size of 200 points. We then added 200 to the minimum (100 points) for pay grade 1 and therefore entered "300" in the "Maximum JE Points" column in the first row. We then entered "500" in the second row, and so on. As you do this, CompSoft calculates the "Minimum JE Points," the "Midpoint JE Points," and the "Actual Midpoint Dollars," based on your pay policy line.

Note that the "equal interval" method is not necessarily the most appropriate method for determining pay grade size in every case. For your system, it may well be that one of the other methods will fit better. Unfortunately, finding out which is the best approach is mainly a trial and error process. You need to try one approach, carry on to develop a pay structure, see how it looks, and then maybe come back and try a different method. In fact, you may have to repeat this process several times. Unfortunately, there is no scientific formula, just informed judgment!

PHASE II - SCREEN 7

CLICK ME FOR INSTRUCTIONS BEFORE PROCEEDING WITH ANY
ACTIVITY ON THIS SCREEN

| Save | Retrieve | | Display Pay Structure Graph |
| Return | | | Next |

Enter the values for the formula y=mx+b (or mx - b) from the Pay Policy Line Graph

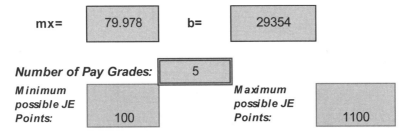

mx=   79.978   b=   29354

Number of Pay Grades: 5

Minimum possible JE Points: 100

Maximum possible JE Points: 1100

Pay Grade	Minimum JE Points	Midpoint JE Points	Maximum JE Points	Actual Midpoint Dollars	Minimum Dollars	Maximum Dollars
1	100	200	300	$45,350	$43,350	$47,350
2	301	400.5	500	$61,385	$57,385	$65,385
3	501	600.5	700	$77,381	$71,381	$83,381
4	701	800.5	900	$93,376	$85,376	$101,376
5	901	1000.5	1100	$109,372	$99,372	$119,372

CompSoft Example
Screen 7

Next, we need to decide on the range spreads. This is the amount above, and the amount below, the "Actual Midpoint Dollars" of the range. Chapter 8 discusses various methods for deciding this. The key thing is to go the <u>same</u> dollar amount above <u>and</u> below the midpoint in each pay grade. If you don't do this, it will skew your entire pay system.

In our example, we arbitrarily decided to go $2000 above and below the midpoint in pay grade 1, $4000 above and below in pay grade 2, $6000 above and below in pay grade 3, $8000 above and below in pay grade 4, and $10000 above and below in pay grade 5. (Note that these amounts are not necessarily based on sound reasoning, although they do adhere to the general principle that pay range spreads should get wider in the higher pay grades.) We calculated the range minimums and maximums for each pay grade based on these amounts, and entered them in the "Minimum dollars" and "Maximum dollars" columns.

Next, we clicked "Display Pay Structure Graph" to produce the graph on the next page.

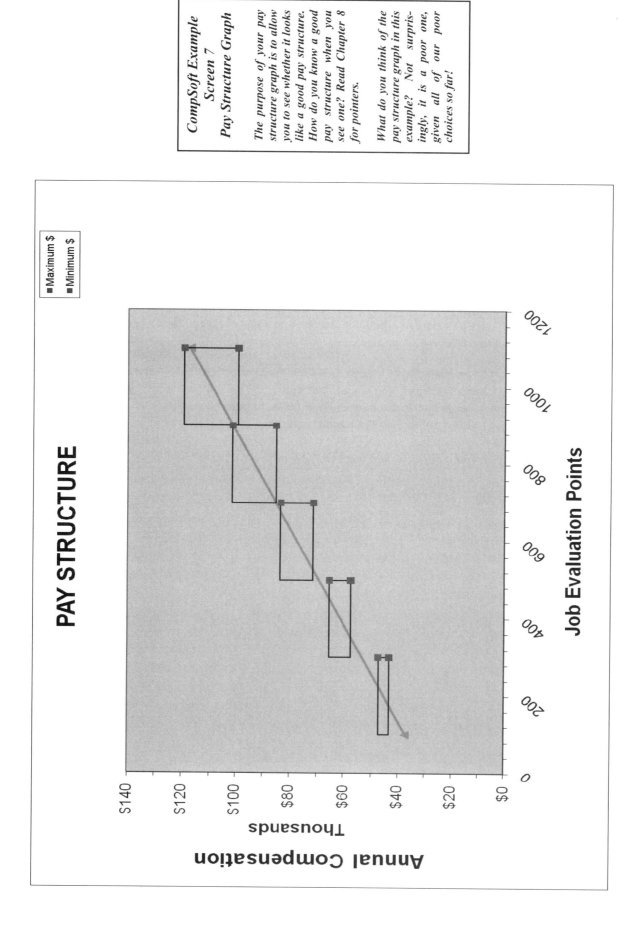

INSTRUCTIONS FOR PHASE II - SCREEN 8 (PRINT THESE INSTRUCTIONS)

1) Your objective in Screen 8 is to allocate each job to a pay grade based on the point total for each job.

2) First, type in the titles of all the jobs in your JE pay structure. After each title, also type (in brackets) the number of JE points that you allocated to that job in Phase I.

3) Based on the JE points for each job, enter the pay grade (from Screen 7) for each job. (After entering a pay grade for every job, click on any other cell to finalize your choices.)

4) Next, click "Get Min, Max, & Mid" and the pay ranges for each job will be automatically displayed.

5) If, in Screen 6, you had the same compensation level (lead, lag, or match) strategy for all jobs in your job evaluation pay structure, click "Save", print your table, and click "Next" to go on to Screen 9.

6) If you have different compensation level (lead, lag, or match) strategies for different jobs in your JE pay structure (and were therefore instructed in Screen 6 to simply enter a "Match" policy), continue on to steps 7 and 8 below.

7) Enter your compensation level strategy for each job in the "% Change" column. For example, if your "Caretaker" job has a 5% lag strategy, enter "-5" in the "% Change" column. If your "Secretary" job has a match strategy, leave the "% Change" column blank. If your "Accountant" has a 10% lead strategy, enter "10" in the "% Change" column.

8) Once you have made all your compensation level adjustments, click "Save", and click "Next".

PHASE II - SCREEN 8

CLICK ME FOR INSTRUCTIONS BEFORE PROCEEDING
WITH ANY ACTIVITIES IN THIS SCREEN

Save

Retrieve

Return

Clear Data

Get Min. Max. & Mid.

Next

Job Title	Pay Grade	Minimum	Midpoint	Maximum	% Change	Adjusted Minimum	Adjusted Midpoint	Adjusted Maximum

PHASE II - SCREEN 8

CLICK ME FOR INSTRUCTIONS BEFORE PROCEEDING
WITH ANY ACTIVITIES IN THIS SCREEN

Save	Retrieve	Get Min. Max. & Mid.	Next
Return	Clear Data		

Job Title	Pay Grade	Minimum	Midpoint	Maximum	% Change	Adjusted Minimum	Adjusted Midpoint	Adjusted Maximum
Caretaker (150 points)	1	$43,350	$45,350	$47,350	-5	$41,183	$43,082	$44,983
Secretary (250 points)	1	$43,350	$45,350	$47,350	-5	$41,183	$43,082	$44,983
Accountant (400 points)	2	$57,385	$61,385	$65,385		$57,385	$61,385	$65,385
Compensation Mgr (450 pts)	2	$57,385	$61,385	$65,385	5	$60,254	$64,454	$68,654
Director of HR (900 points)	4	$85,376	$93,376	$101,376	5	$89,645	$98,045	$106,445

CompSoft Example
Screen 8

In Screen 8, first type in the titles of all your jobs under your job evaluation pay structure, along with their JE point scores, in brackets. (In the example here, we just typed in the five jobs we have been working with, but you need to include all your JE jobs, not just your bench-mark jobs.)

Then, from the pay structure you created in Screen 7, identify the pay grade that each job falls into, based on its JE points score. Type in the number of the pay grade for each job. Then click on "Get Min. Max. & Mid." This fills in the dollar figures for each job.

If you are using a constant pay level strategy, move on to Screen 9 now. If you are using a differential pay level strategy, you enter the lead or lag percentages (from your compensation strategy templates) for each job in the "% Change" column, as we have done here.

-90-

PHASE II - SCREEN 9

1) Your objective in Screen 9 is to apply your compensation mix strategy (from your compensation strategy templates in Phase I) to your job evaluation pay structure.

2) For each job title, enter the percentage of total compensation that each pay component is expected to provide. CompSoft will automatically calculate the ranges for each of these components for each job.

3) You have now finished developing your job evaluation pay structure (Section H of the compensation project).

4) Print this table, click "Save", and click "Finish". Congratulate yourselves on finishing this heavy section, but don't forget about Sections I and J!

CHECK SYSTEM MESSAGES COLUMN

[Return]   [Save]   [Finish]

Job Title	Pay Grade	Base Pay			Ind. Perf. Pay			Group Perf. Pay			Org. Perf. Pay			Indirect Pay			Total Compensation	
		% TC	Minimum	Maximum	% TC	Minimum	Maximum	% TC	Minimum	Maximum	% TC	Minimum	Maximum	% TC	Minimum	Maximum	Minimum	Maximum
Caretaker (150 points)	1																$41,183	$44,983
Secretary (250 points)	1																$41,183	$44,983
Accountant (400 points)	2																$57,385	$65,385
Compensation Mgr (450 pts)	2																$60,254	$68,654
Director of HR (900 points)	4																$89,645	$106,445

CompSoft Example
Screen 9

When you click on "Next" after finishing Screen 8, CompSoft automatically pulls your total compensation range for each job into Screen 9. All that remains for us is to refer to our compensation strategy templates from Phase I to identify the proportions of total compensation that each pay component is projected to comprise in the compensation package for each job, and enter them in the shaded columns. CompSoft will automatically calculate the dollar amounts of the ranges for each pay component for each job. Once you have done this, you will have developed a compensation structure for all of your jobs under your JE system, and you are ready to move on. Take pride in reaching this difficult milestone! But don't forget about Sections I and J!

Phase III – Operationalizing the Compensation System

Your mission for Phase III of the project is to do three main things. First, flesh out your performance pay and indirect pay plans. Second, apply your new pay structure to current employees of the client firm. Third, develop procedures for implementation and ongoing management of the compensation system.

To successfully accomplish Phase III, you will need to have read and utilized appropriate concepts from Chapters 10 to 13 and the "Applying Job Evaluation Results" section of Chapter 7. When preparing your report, use the following five headings, and the same letters for your tabs.

Phase III Report Headings

Section K: Performance Pay Plans. In this section, you need to take each of the performance pay plans that you are recommending, and describe the key characteristics of each, as they will be applied at your client firm. For example, if you have a profit sharing plan, who will be eligible, what proportion of profits will be allocated to the plan, what will be the form of the payout (e.g., current or deferred; cash or stock), how often will it pay out, and how it will be allocated across eligible employees are just some of the questions you need to address. In so doing, you always need to provide your underlying rationale for your choices. Also, discuss the possible advantages the plan may produce, and the possible disadvantages that may arise. Chapter 11 identifies the key issues in designing the main types of performance pay plans. But don't forget that if you have a merit pay plan that depends on appraised employee performance (as most teams will have as part of their movement through the pay range policy developed in Phase II), then you need to develop a performance appraisal system, as described in Chapter 10.

Section L: Indirect Pay Plan. You also need to describe the characteristics of your indirect pay plan. Some of the questions to be addressed include the following: Will it be a fixed, flexible, or semi-flexible plan? Which benefits will be included? Will some benefits be contributory? Will the same features apply to all employees? In so doing, you need to provide the rationale for the choices you make, as well as a discussion of the advantages you think the plan will produce, and possible disadvantages. Chapter 12 provides the necessary foundation of knowledge for this.

Section M: Application of Your New Pay Structure. In this section, you will apply your new pay structure to sixty current employees of your client firm. You need to bring their compensation into line with the new system, indicating how you would deal with each specific employee. Following up on your discussion of this issue in Phase II, you need to develop specific criteria and procedures for adjusting the compensation of employees who do not currently fit into your new pay structure. (As you will recall, Chapter 7 discusses this issue.) You need also to take whatever human resource actions are necessary (e.g., terminations, retirements, transfers, promotions) and authorize the hiring of any necessary new employees. Provide your rationale for all actions you take. Include printouts of Screens 2 and 3 in this section.

Section N: Recommended Compensation Budget. The outcome of all the previous steps is a recommended compensation budget for the coming year. Compare this with the current expenditures, and explain why your new budget will be advantageous to the company. At the same time, discuss any possible downsides or risks in adopting your recommended budget.

In so doing, remember to take the structure (not just the total cost) of your new compensation system into account. For example, if organizational performance pay accounts for a large portion of your total compensation, remember that these plans will only pay out if company performance is good. The same is true, although to a lesser extent, for group and individual performance pay.

There are many things you could do in this section. For example, you could do some projections of various revenue scenarios for the next two years. If revenues stayed the same for the next two years, what would happen to profits under your new compensation system? What would happen if the old compensation system is simply carried forward? What would happen to profits if revenue went up by 10%? What if revenues went down by 10%?

The section "Evaluating the Compensation System" in Chapter 13 should give you some ideas of what you could do here. Include a printout of Screen 4 in this section.

Finally, note that when you discuss what the annual compensation costs will be under your new system, you need to multiply your "recommended compensation budget" by 20 if your client is Duplox Copiers, or by 10 if your client is Zenith Medical Systems. The reason is that you have applied your new compensation system to only 5% of Duplox employees, and 10% of Zenith employees, so you need to adjust your "recommended compensation budget" to account for that.

Section O: Implementation and Ongoing Management of the Compensation System. In this section, you need to describe your procedures for implementing your new system, as well as for the ongoing management of the system. Many good plans fail due to poor implementation, and many good plans can become ineffective if not managed properly over time. The issues discussed in Chapter 13 need to be addressed in this section.

CompSoft (Phase III) Screens

Following are printouts of the CompSoft screens that you will be using in Phase III. Two sets are provided. The first set applies if your client firm is Duplox Copiers Canada Limited. The second set applies if your client firm is Zenith Medical Systems Incorporated. When you are doing Phase III, be sure that you are using the software file that pertains to your client firm!

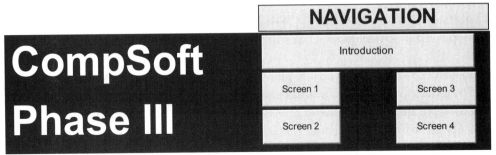

Compensation Simulation Software (4th Edition, 2010)

(For use with Duplox Copiers Canada Limited only)

To accompany Richard J. Long's *Strategic Compensation in Canada* published by Nelson Education, Toronto, 4th Edition, 2010.

Software Development:

Henry Ravichander, BSc, DBM, AGS (USA), MBA (Can)
Sessional Lecturer
Edwards School of Business
University of Saskatchewan
ravichander@edwards.usask.ca

GENERAL INSTRUCTIONS FOR PHASE III

Your objective in Phase III of this project is to do three main things:

1) Flesh out the details of your performance pay and indirect pay plans.

2) Apply your new pay structure to current employees of the firm. In so doing, you will take any human resource actions necessary (i.e., termination, retirement, transfer, promotion) and also budget for any necessary new employees. The result of this step is a recommended compensation budget for the coming year.

3) Develop methods for implementation and ongoing management of the compensation system.

CompSoft is designed to help you with Step 2 of this phase.

Note: When saving your CompSoft file on Excel, DO NOT alter the name of the file in any way! This can cause unpredictable consequences.

Phase III - Screen 1

1) This is the actual compensation of current employees of the firm.

2) Performance ratings are as follows:
   1 - Exceeds standards in all job requirments
   2 - Exceeds standards in most job requirements
   3 - Meets standards in all job requirements
   4 - Fails to meet standards in some job requirements
   5 - Fails to meet standards in most job requirements

3) If a "0" appears in the "Years With Firm", "Years In Job" or "Performance Rating" columns, this means that the employee has less than one year's service, and no performance rating has been done.

Next   Return

Emp. #	Emp. Name	Job Title	Age	Gender	Yrs. With Firm	Yrs. In Job	Perf. Rating	Current Base Pay	Current Ind. Perf. Pay	Current Grp. Perf. Pay	Current Org. Perf. Pay	Current Indirect Pay	Current Total Comp.
1	Sereena Albers	TSS I-Model 2000	23	F	1	1	3	$26,180	$0	$0	$0	$4,620	$30,800
2	Joel Bartsch	Field Service Manager	46	M	10	5	1	$46,475	$14,300	$0	$0	$10,725	$71,500
3	Conor Baynton	TSS II - Model 4000	30	M	0	0	0	$38,335	$0	$0	$0	$6,765	$45,100
4	Armand Bell	Branch Inventory Clerk	24	M	4	2	4	$24,310	$0	$0	$0	$4,290	$28,600
5	Lester Briley	TSS I - Model 2000	22	M	0	0	0	$27,115	$0	$0	$0	$4,785	$31,900
6	Sara Callbeck-Jenson	Compensation Manage	30	F	10	5	3	$65,450	$0	$0	$0	$11,550	$77,000
7	Colin Chell	TSS I-Model 1000	26	M	3	3	4	$30,855	$0	$0	$0	$5,445	$36,300
8	Nick Crooks	Field Service Manager	45	M	20	5	3	$42,900	$13,200	$0	$0	$9,900	$66,000
9	Roger Cross	TSS I - Model 4000	25	M	2	2	2	$28,050	$0	$0	$0	$4,950	$33,000
10	Sandi Dekker	Compensation Officer	28	F	0	0	0	$46,750	$0	$0	$0	$8,250	$55,000
11	Daniel Dewar	TSS II - Model 2000	26	M	4	1	3	$32,725	$0	$0	$0	$5,775	$38,500
12	Keith Dickie	Branch Service Manag	50	M	30	15	1	$49,500	$20,625	$0	$0	$12,375	$82,500
13	Katie Downing	Sales Representative	31	F	6	6	3	$33,000	$22,633	$0	$0	$9,818	$65,450
14	Marvin Dzaka	TSS II - Model 3000	28	M	5	4	4	$33,660	$0	$0	$0	$5,940	$39,600
15	Kerry Edeen	Dir. Tech. Services	50	M	25	8	3	$110,000	$34,925	$0	$0	$25,575	$170,500
16	Wayne Epp	TSS II - Model 2000	24	M	2	1	1	$31,790	$0	$0	$0	$5,610	$37,400
17	Rhonda Guinan	Sales Training Spec.	42	F	15	10	3	$72,050	$0	$0	$0	$11,550	$83,600
18	Chad Gusikoski	Sales Representative	30	M	8	8	3	$33,000	$25,905	$0	$0	$10,395	$69,300
19	Karen Haubrich	Sales Representative	32	F	5	5	3	$33,000	$20,295	$0	$0	$9,405	$62,700
20	Marcia Hicks	Regional Sales Manag	60	F	35	10	2	$49,500	$34,650	$0	$0	$14,850	$99,000

#	Name	Position	Age	Sex									
21	Wilmer Isbister	Sales Representative	38	M	12	12	2	$33,000	$30,580	$0	$0	$11,220	$74,800
22	Cal Jamieson	TSS II - Model 3000	26	M	4	2	3	$33,660	$0	$0	$0	$5,940	$39,600
23	Heather Keller	Dir. Tech. Training/Sup	32	F	2	2	3	$85,800	$26,400	$0	$0	$19,800	$132,000
24	Carlene King	TSS II - Model 1000	25	F	3	1	2	$32,725	$0	$0	$0	$5,775	$38,500
25	Amos Korte	TSS III - Model 3000	28	M	6	2	2	$42,075	$0	$0	$0	$7,425	$49,500
26	Dennis Kranz	Branch Service Manag	40	M	15	5	4	$49,500	$14,850	$0	$0	$11,550	$75,900
27	Jeff Kreese	Mgr. Branch Inventorie	28	M	2	2	2	$50,050	$3,080	$0	$0	$11,550	$64,680
28	Shana Laird	Dir. Human Resources	55	F	5	5	4	$123,200	$7,700	$0	$0	$23,100	$154,000
29	Clarence Lau	Caretaker	20	M	1	1	2	$19,635	$0	$0	$0	$3,465	$23,100
30	Janice Larson	TSS III - Model 2000	29	F	6	2	1	$39,270	$0	$0	$0	$6,930	$46,200
31	Sharla Lee	Sales Representative	35	F	5	5	3	$33,000	$18,425	$0	$0	$9,075	$60,500
32	Carl Loney-Tindall	TSS III - Model 3000	28	M	6	0	0	$39,270	$0	$0	$0	$6,930	$46,200
33	Morty McGregor	Accountant	40	M	5	5	3	$60,775	$0	$0	$0	$10,725	$71,500
34	Andrew Miller	TSS III - Model 3000	42	M	0	0	0	$43,945	$0	$0	$0	$7,755	$51,700
35	Jerry Mushka	TSS I - Model 2000	25	M	2	2	3	$28,985	$0	$0	$0	$5,115	$34,100
36	Lyle Neufeld	TSS III - Model 4000	48	M	24	21	1	$56,100	$0	$0	$0	$9,900	$66,000
37	James Nesdoly	TSS III - Model 1000	46	M	22	18	4	$56,100	$0	$0	$0	$9,900	$66,000
38	Lawrence Oborowsky	Sales Representative	40	M	10	10	3	$33,000	$23,100	$0	$0	$9,900	$66,000
39	Colin Okrainetz	Sales Representative	45	M	20	20	2	$33,000	$27,775	$0	$0	$10,725	$71,500
40	Nick Onufreychuk	TSS II - Model 4000	28	M	5	1	4	$35,530	$0	$0	$0	$6,270	$41,800
41	Nathan Parnetta	Sales Representative	30	M	2	2	4	$33,000	$13,750	$0	$0	$8,250	$55,000
42	Barbara Redekopp	Inventory Clerk	22	F	2	2	2	$20,570	$0	$0	$0	$3,630	$24,200
43	Erin Richards	Advert. & Promo. Spec	32	F	6	3	2	$56,100	$0	$0	$0	$9,900	$66,000
44	Al Ritchie	Field Service Manager	58	M	35	30	4	$51,480	$9,295	$0	$0	$10,725	$71,500
45	Sean Robertson	TSS II - Model 3000	31	M	1	1	5	$37,400	$0	$0	$0	$6,600	$44,000
46	Cheryl Schroeder	TSS III - Model 4000	33	F	9	4	3	$42,075	$0	$0	$0	$7,425	$49,500
47	Marv Shutiak	Training/Support Spec	48	M	20	18	4	$66,385	$0	$0	$0	$11,715	$78,100
48	Darcy Simpson	Secretary	62	F	40	40	3	$39,270	$0	$0	$0	$6,930	$46,200
49	Kim Slimmon	Director of Marketing	50	F	25	5	1	$99,000	$59,950	$0	$0	$28,050	$187,000
50	Carson Stadnyk	Field Service Manager	40	M	8	2	2	$38,280	$15,950	$0	$0	$9,570	$63,800
51	Victor Stang	TSS II - Model 2000	27	M	4	2	1	$37,400	$0	$0	$0	$6,600	$44,000
52	Colleen Steele	Compensation Clerk	26	F	5	1	4	$28,050	$0	$0	$0	$4,950	$33,000
53	Deanna Tamke	Sales Representative	26	F	4	4	5	$33,000	$15,620	$0	$0	$8,580	$57,200
54	Heather Taylor	TSS II - Model 1000	30	F	5	3	3	$35,530	$0	$0	$0	$6,270	$41,800
55	Raymond Weatherald	TSS III - Model 2000	45	M	3	3	3	$46,750	$0	$0	$0	$8,250	$55,000
56	Ray White	Caretaker	28	M	5	5	4	$22,440	$0	$0	$0	$3,960	$26,400
57	Eddie Will	TSS III - Model 4000	50	M	26	23	4	$51,425	$0	$0	$0	$9,075	$60,500
58	John Wilson	Sales Representative	48	M	22	22	1	$33,000	$32,450	$0	$0	$11,550	$77,000
59	Bernard Yam	TSS III - Model 1000	38	M	15	11	3	$51,425	$0	$0	$0	$9,075	$60,500
60	Julia Zbaraschuk	Branch Sales Manage	35	F	13	3	3	$44,000	$30,800	$0	$0	$13,200	$88,000
No. of Emps.on Payroll:	60	COLUMN TOTALS						$2,649,845	$516,258	$0	$0	$559,928	$3,726,030

Phase III - Screen 2

1) Your objective in this screen is to summarize the decisions you have made in applying your new pay structure to current employees.
2) For each employee, put in the job title they will have, and all the relevant compensation information.
3) For any employee that you are firing, put in "Terminated" in the "Job Title" column, or "Retired" for any employees who will retire. Then enter "0" for fields with column headers shaded green.
4) Enter the data only in the areas that are shaded grey.
5) Click "Save" to store the new data that you have entered.
6) Click "Retrieve" to restore any data that you have previously saved.
7) Scroll down to see the impact of your decisions in this screen.
8) If you want to restore all the old job titles, click the "Restore Old Job Titles".
9) Once satisfied with your data, click "Next" to move to Screen 3.

Save		Retrieve		Restore Old Job Titles		Next		Return

Emp. #	Emp. Name	Job Title	Pay Grade	New Minimum	New Maximum	Current Base Pay	New Base Pay	Current Ind. Perf. Pay	New Ind. Perf. Pay	Current Grp. Perf. Pay	New Grp. Perf. Pay	Current Org. Perf. Pay	New Org. Perf. Pay	Current Indirect Pay	New Indirect Pay	Current Total Comp.	New Total Comp.
1	Sereena Albers	Secretary				$26,180		$0		$0		$0		$4,620		$30,800	
2	Joel Bartsch	Secretary				$46,475		$14,300		$0		$0		$10,725		$71,500	
3	Conor Baynton	Int Apps Prog - MMS				$38,335		$0		$0		$0		$6,765		$45,100	
4	Armand Bell	Sr Apps Prog - RS				$24,310		$0		$0		$0		$4,290		$28,600	
5	Lester Briley	Jr Apps Prog - MMS				$27,115		$0		$0		$0		$4,785		$31,900	
6	Sara Callbeck-Jenson	Int Apps Prog - MTS				$65,450		$0		$0		$0		$11,550		$77,000	
7	Colin Chell	Int Apps Prog - SS				$30,855		$0		$0		$0		$5,445		$36,300	
8	Nick Crooks	Jr Apps Prog - RS				$42,900		$13,200		$0		$0		$9,900		$66,000	
9	Roger Cross	Jr Apps Prog - FMS				$28,050		$0		$0		$0		$4,950		$33,000	
10	Sandi Dekker	Sr Apps Prog - FMS				$46,750		$0		$0		$0		$8,250		$55,000	
11	Danie Dewar	Sr Apps Prog - FMS				$32,725		$0		$0		$0		$5,775		$38,500	
12	Keith Dickie	Jr Apps Prog - MTS				$49,500		$20,625		$0		$0		$12,375		$82,500	
13	Katie Downing	Int Apps Prog - MMS				$33,000		$22,633		$0		$0		$9,818		$65,450	
14	Marvin Dzaka	Jr Apps Prog - FMS				$33,660		$0		$0		$0		$5,940		$39,600	
15	Kerry Edeen	Reg Marketing Mgr				$110,000		$34,925		$0		$0		$25,575		$170,500	
16	Wayne Epp	Dir Systems Dev				$31,790		$0		$0		$0		$5,610		$37,400	
17	Rhonca Guinan	Sys Marketing Spec				$72,050		$0		$0		$0		$11,550		$83,600	
18	Chad Gusikoski	Jr Apps Prog - RS				$33,000		$25,905		$0		$0		$10,395		$69,300	
19	Karen Haubrich	Sr Apps Prog - MTS				$33,000		$20,295		$0		$0		$9,405		$62,700	
20	Marcia Hicks	Int Apps Prog - RS				$49,500		$34,650		$0		$0		$14,850		$99,000	

#	Name	Title								
21	Wilmer Isbister	Compensation Clerk	$33,000	$0	$30,580	$0	$0	$11,220	$0	$74,800
22	Cal Jamieson	Sys Marketing Spec	$33,660	$0	$0	$0	$0	$5,940	$0	$39,600
23	Heather Keller	Jr Apps Prog - SS	$85,800	$0	$26,400	$0	$0	$19,800	$0	$132,000
24	Carlene King	Caretaker	$32,725	$0	$0	$0	$0	$5,775	$0	$38,500
25	Amos Korte	Accountant	$42,075	$0	$0	$0	$0	$7,425	$0	$49,500
26	Dennis Kranz	Jr Apps Prog - MMS	$49,500	$0	$14,850	$0	$0	$11,550	$0	$75,900
27	Jeff Kreese	Sr Apps Prog - MTS	$50,050	$0	$3,080	$0	$0	$11,550	$0	$64,680
28	Shana Laird	Compensation Clerk	$123,200	$0	$7,700	$0	$0	$23,100	$0	$154,000
29	Clarence Lau	Compensation Clerk	$19,635	$0	$0	$0	$0	$3,465	$0	$23,100
30	Janice Larson	Sr Apps Prog - MMS	$39,270	$0	$0	$0	$0	$6,930	$0	$46,200
31	Sharla Lee	Dir Human Resources	$33,000	$0	$18,425	$0	$0	$9,075	$0	$60,500
32	Carl Loney-Tindall	Sys Integration Spec	$39,270	$0	$0	$0	$0	$6,930	$0	$46,200
33	Morty McGregor	Int Apps Prog - FMS	$60,775	$0	$0	$0	$0	$10,725	$0	$71,500
34	Andrew Miller	Jr Systems Trainer	$43,945	$0	$0	$0	$0	$7,755	$0	$51,700
35	Jerry Mushka	Sr Sys Install Spec	$28,985	$0	$0	$0	$0	$5,115	$0	$34,100
36	Lyle Neufeld	Sr Apps Prog - SS	$56,100	$0	$0	$0	$0	$9,900	$0	$66,000
37	James Nesdoly	Int Apps Prog - SS	$56,100	$0	$0	$0	$0	$9,900	$0	$66,000
38	Lawrence Oborowsky	Reg Marketing Mgr	$33,000	$0	$23,100	$0	$0	$9,900	$0	$66,000
39	Colin Okrainetz	Sr Sys HW Analyst	$33,000	$0	$27,775	$0	$0	$10,725	$0	$71,500
40	Nick Onufreychuk	Jr Apps Prog - SS	$35,530	$0	$0	$0	$0	$6,270	$0	$41,800
41	Nathan Parnetta	Int Apps Prog - FMS	$33,000	$0	$13,750	$0	$0	$8,250	$0	$55,000
42	Barbara Redekopp	Sys Integration Spec	$20,570	$0	$0	$0	$0	$3,630	$0	$24,200
43	Erin Richards	Sys Marketing Spec	$56,100	$0	$0	$0	$0	$9,900	$0	$66,000
44	Al Ritchie	Int Apps Prog - MMS	$51,480	$0	$9,295	$0	$0	$10,725	$0	$71,500
45	Sean Robertson	Sys Design Analyst	$37,400	$0	$0	$0	$0	$6,600	$0	$44,000
46	Cheryl Schroeder	Compensation Officer	$42,075	$0	$0	$0	$0	$7,425	$0	$49,500
47	Marv Shutiak	Sr Apps Prog - RS	$66,385	$0	$0	$0	$0	$11,715	$0	$78,100
48	Darcy Simpson	Int Apps Prog - RS	$39,270	$0	$0	$0	$0	$6,930	$0	$46,200
49	Kim Slimmon	Sys Design Analyst	$99,000	$0	$59,950	$0	$0	$28,050	$0	$187,000
50	Carson Stadnyk	Accountant	$38,280	$0	$15,950	$0	$0	$9,570	$0	$63,800
51	Victor Stang	Jr Systems Trainer	$37,400	$0	$0	$0	$0	$6,600	$0	$44,000
52	Colleen Steele	Caretaker	$28,050	$0	$0	$0	$0	$4,950	$0	$33,000
53	Deanna Tamke	Compensation Mgr	$33,000	$0	$15,620	$0	$0	$8,580	$0	$57,200
54	Heather Taylor	Dir Marketing	$35,530	$0	$0	$0	$0	$6,270	$0	$41,800
55	Raymond Weatherald	Sys Marketing Spec	$46,750	$0	$0	$0	$0	$8,250	$0	$55,000
56	Ray White	Sr Sys HW Analyst	$22,440	$0	$0	$0	$0	$3,960	$0	$26,400
57	Eddie Will	Jr Apps Prog - MTS	$51,425	$0	$0	$0	$0	$9,075	$0	$60,500
58	John Wilson	Mgr - FMS Dev	$33,000	$0	$32,450	$0	$0	$11,550	$0	$77,000
59	Bernard Yam	Sr Sys Install Spec	$51,425	$0	$0	$0	$0	$9,075	$0	$60,500
60	Julia Zbaraschuk	Sr Apps Prog - SS	$44,000	$0	$30,800	$0	$0	$13,200	$0	$88,000
	COLUMN TOTALS		$2,649,845	$0	$516,258	$0	$0	$559,928	$0	$3,726,030

No. of Emps. on Payroll: 60

Phase III - Screen 3

1) If you are planning to hire any new employees, fill their projected compensation information in the areas shaded grey.
2) Click "Save" to store the information you have entered.
3) Click "Retrieve" to restore any data that you have previously saved in this screen.
4) Click "Next" to go to Screen 4.

| Save | Retrieve | Next | Return |

Emp. #	Emp. Name	Job Title	Pay Grade	Base Pay	Ind. Perf. Pay	Grp. Perf. Pay	Org. Perf. Pay	Indirect Pay	New Total Comp.
TOTALS				$0	$0	$0	$0	$0	$0

No. of New Hires: 0

Phase III - Screen 4

1) This screen simply summarizes your recommended compensation budget for the coming year, and compares it to the current year.

2) Review this information and reflect on whether these results will maximize the success of the company.

3) Click Excel's "Save" icon to save the workbook.

4) Once satisfied, click "Finish".

[Return]   [Finish]

RECOMMENDED COMPENSATION BUDGET

Description	No. of Emps.	Base Pay	Ind. Perf. Pay	Grp. Perf. Pay	Org. Perf. Pay	Indirect Pay	Total Comp.
Recommended Compensation Totals (From Screen 2)	60	$0	$0	$0	$0	$0	$0
New Hire Compensation Totals (From Screen 3)	0	$0	$0	$0	$0	$0	$0
Recommended Compensation Budget	60	$0	$0	$0	$0	$0	$0
Current Compensation Totals (From Screen 1)	60	$2,649,845	$516,258	$0	$0	$559,928	$3,726,030
Employment Increase/Decrease (Compared to Current Compensation Totals in Screen 1)							0.00%
Budget Increase/Decrease (Compared to Current Compensation Totals in Screen 1)							0.00%

CompSoft Phase III

NAVIGATION

Introduction

Screen 1   Screen 3

Screen 2   Screen 4

Compensation Simulation Software (4th Edition, 2010)

(For use with Zenith Medical Systems Incorporated only)

To accompany Richard J. Long's *Strategic Compensation in Canada* published by Nelson Education, Toronto, 4th Edition, 2010.

Software Development:

Henry Ravichander, BSc, DBM, AGS (USA), MBA (Sask)
Sessional Lecturer
Edwards School of Business
University of Saskatchewan

GENERAL INSTRUCTIONS FOR PHASE III

Your objective in Phase III of this project is to do three main things:

1) Flesh out the details of your performance pay and indirect pay plans.

2) Apply your new pay structure to current employees of the firm. In so doing, you will take any human resource actions necessary (i.e., termination, retirement, transfer, promotion) and also budget for any necessary new employees. The result of this step is a recommended compensation budget for the coming year.

3) Develop methods for implementation and ongoing management of the compensation system.

 CompSoft is designed to help you with Step 2 of this phase.

Note: When saving your CompSoft file on Excel, DO NOT alter the name of the file in any way! This can cause unpredictable consequences.

Phase III - Screen 1

1) This is the actual compensation of current employees of the firm.

2) Performance ratings are as follows:
   1 - Exceeds standards in all job requirments
   2 - Exceeds standards in most job requirements
   3 - Meets standards in all job requirements
   4 - Fails to meet standards in some job requirements
   5 - Fails to meet standards in most job requirements

3) If a "0" appears in the "Years With Firm", "Years In Job" or "Performance Rating" columns, this means that the employee has less than one year's service, and no performance rating has been done.

Next   Return

Emp. #	Emp. Name	Job Title	Age	Gender	Yrs. With Firm	Yrs. In Job	Perf. Rating	Current Base Pay	Current Ind. Perf. Pay	Current Grp. Perf. Pay	Current Org. Perf. Pay	Current Indirect Pay	Current Total Comp.
1	Affleck, Jen	Secretary	36	F	10	6	5	$29,423	$0	$0	$0	$13,147	$42,570
2	Aurat, Neha	Secretary	62	F	30	25	3	$36,667	$0	$0	$0	$16,463	$53,130
3	Avinashi, Connor	Int Apps Prog - MMS	29	M	4	3	1	$44,561	$0	$0	$0	$20,119	$64,680
4	Berg, Jim	Sr Apps Prog - RS	35	M	10	6	3	$63,206	$0	$0	$0	$28,534	$91,740
5	Boehm, Nick	Jr Apps Prog - MMS	24	M	0	0	0	$33,946	$0	$0	$0	$15,004	$48,950
6	Borycki, Al	Int Apps Prog - MTS	27	F	0	0	0	$41,745	$0	$0	$0	$18,755	$60,500
7	Breitkruz, Lee	Int Apps Prog - SS	27	M	1	1	1	$42,504	$0	$0	$0	$19,096	$61,600
8	Brown, Tracy	Jr Apps Prog - RS	27	F	2	2	5	$36,432	$0	$0	$0	$16,368	$52,800
9	Brucks, Craig	Jr Apps Prog - FMS	24	M	1	1	2	$34,914	$0	$0	$0	$15,686	$50,600
10	Chan, Wing	Sr Apps Prog - FMS	31	M	6	3	5	$59,202	$0	$0	$0	$26,598	$85,800
11	Chau, Yong	Sr Apps Prog - FMS	30	M	5	2	1	$57,684	$0	$0	$0	$25,916	$83,600
12	Cherniske, Amy	Jr Apps Prog - MTS	26	F	3	3	4	$37,950	$0	$0	$0	$17,050	$55,000
13	Chin, Kwok	Int Apps Prog - MMS	27	M	2	1	3	$43,263	$0	$0	$0	$19,437	$62,700
14	Cirkvencic, Cindy	Jr Apps Prog - FMS	23	F	0	0	0	$33,726	$0	$0	$0	$15,224	$48,950
15	Coleman, Trevor	Reg Marketing Mgr	29	M	6	1	2	$43,076	$5,500	$0	$0	$21,824	$70,400
16	Cozac, Terry	Dir Systems Dev	58	M	32	0	0	$143,000	$46,750	$0	$0	$63,250	$253,000
17	Croissant, Dustin	Sys Marketing Spec	27	M	1	1	3	$24,552	$6,567	$0	$0	$13,981	$45,100
18	Currie, Ashton	Jr Apps Prog - RS	24	M	1	1	3	$34,914	$0	$0	$0	$15,686	$50,600
19	Dithavong, Mandu	Sr Apps Prog - MTS	38	M	12	6	3	$63,756	$0	$0	$0	$28,644	$92,400
20	Dorgan, Jolene	Int Apps Prog - RS	33	F	5	3	4	$46,299	$0	$0	$0	$20,801	$67,100

#	Name	Title	Age	Sex									
21	Edmondson, Nola	Compensation Clerk	32	F	2	2	3	$28,842	$0	$0	$0	$12,958	$41,800
22	Freiheit, Laurel	Sys Marketing Spec	29	F	2	2	4	$26,752	$12,716	$0	$0	$17,732	$57,200
23	Gandhi, Jawah	Jr Apps Prog - SS	23	M	0	0	0	$33,396	$0	$0	$0	$15,004	$48,400
24	Gargol, Walter	Caretaker	36	M	1	1	4	$22,011	$0	$0	$0	$9,889	$31,900
25	Guenther, Michelle	Accountant	30	F	5	5	4	$47,058	$0	$0	$0	$21,142	$68,200
26	Hitchings, Ashford	Jr Apps Prog - MMS	25	M	2	2	3	$36,432	$0	$0	$0	$16,368	$52,800
27	Jakubiec, Chris E.	Sr Apps Prog - MTS	36	M	8	4	4	$60,720	$0	$0	$0	$27,280	$88,000
28	Johns, Jessica	Compensation Clerk	60	F	30	8	4	$33,396	$0	$0	$0	$15,004	$48,400
29	Kalra, Suresh	Sr Apps Prog - MMS	34	M	4	1	3	$56,166	$0	$0	$0	$25,234	$81,400
30	Kane, Kristie	Dir Human Resources	48	F	25	2	4	$115,500	$0	$0	$0	$38,500	$154,000
31	Khosla, Raj	Sys Integration Spec	41	M	15	6	5	$67,551	$0	$0	$0	$30,349	$97,900
32	Kumar, Kalburgi	Int Apps Prog - FMS	28	M	3	1	3	$44,022	$0	$0	$0	$19,778	$63,800
33	Laing, Patricia	Jr Systems Trainer	26	F	1	1	3	$32,258	$0	$0	$0	$14,493	$46,750
34	Leach, Tommy	Sr Sys Install Spec	37	M	2	2	2	$55,407	$0	$0	$0	$24,893	$80,300
35	Loblaw, Cora	Sr Apps Prog - SS	32	F	9	4	2	$60,720	$0	$0	$0	$27,280	$88,000
36	Ludu, Pradeep	Int Apps Prog - SS	28	M	4	0	4	$43,263	$0	$0	$0	$19,437	$62,700
37	Matsalla, Joe D.	Reg Marketing Mgr	31	M	8	2	0	$46,684	$11,000	$0	$0	$25,916	$83,600
38	Matshes, Jay	Sr Sys HW Analyst	31	M	2	2	3	$59,961	$0	$0	$0	$26,939	$86,900
39	McQueen, Derrick	Jr Apps Prog - SS	28	M	5	5	2	$40,986	$0	$0	$0	$18,414	$59,400
40	Miller, Dean	Int Apps Prog - FMS	26	M	0	0	0	$41,745	$0	$0	$0	$18,755	$60,500
41	Nesbit, Roger	Sys Integration Spec	38	M	13	1	1	$62,238	$0	$0	$0	$27,962	$90,200
42	Paluck, Darren	Sys Marketing Spec	30	M	2	2	4	$26,752	$16,522	$0	$0	$19,096	$62,370
43	Pappadanis, Ari	Sr Apps Prog - MMS	35	M	9	5	2	$62,238	$0	$0	$0	$27,962	$90,200
44	Rammaya, Anuj	Int Apps Prog - MTS	32	M	7	5	2	$47,817	$0	$0	$0	$21,483	$69,300
45	Rans, Scot	Sys Design Analyst	33	M	8	1	1	$56,166	$0	$0	$0	$25,234	$81,400
46	Rezansoff, Erin	Compensation Officer	28	F	2	2	5	$31,119	$0	$0	$0	$13,981	$45,100
47	Ripley, Thomas	Sr Apps Prog - RS	29	M	1	1	3	$56,166	$0	$0	$0	$25,234	$81,400
48	Selensky, Alwyn	Int Apps Prog - RS	29	M	4	2	5	$44,022	$0	$0	$0	$19,778	$63,800
49	Shumaker, Gavin	Sys Design Analyst	29	M	4	2	5	$50,116	$0	$0	$0	$22,506	$72,622
50	Simpson, Fred	Accountant	26	M	2	2	2	$42,504	$0	$0	$0	$19,096	$61,600
51	Sproule, Natalia	Jr Systems Trainer	24	F	2	2	3	$33,396	$0	$0	$0	$15,004	$48,400
52	Stadnyk, Darren	Caretaker	40	M	2	2	2	$22,770	$0	$0	$0	$10,230	$33,000
53	Stewart, Stephanie	Compensation Mgr	30	F	8	2	4	$41,745	$0	$0	$0	$18,755	$60,500
54	Stefaniuk, Michelle	Dir Marketing	51	F	26	2	3	$121,000	$11,000	$0	$0	$44,000	$176,000
55	Sundby, Reid	Sys Marketing Spec	26	M	1	1	3	$24,552	$8,085	$0	$0	$14,663	$47,300
56	Wapriaski, Stacey	Sr Sys HW Analyst	34	F	6	4	4	$61,479	$0	$0	$0	$27,621	$89,100
57	Wong, Alvin	Jr Apps Prog - MTS	26	M	3	3	3	$37,950	$0	$0	$0	$17,050	$55,000
58	Wong, Sheldon	Mgr - FMS Dev	42	M	20	8	4	$99,550	$0	$0	$0	$33,000	$132,550
59	Wormsbecker, Dan	Sr Sys Install Spec	33	M	8	2	3	$57,904	$0	$0	$0	$25,916	$83,820
60	Wu, Tong	Sr Apps Prog - SS	29	M	0	0	0	$55,198	$0	$0	$0	$24,552	$79,750
	No. of Emps. on Payroll: 60	**COLUMN TOTALS**						$2,938,372	$118,140	$0	$0	$1,310,070	$4,366,582

Phase III - Screen 2

1) Your objective in this screen is to summarize the decisions you have made in applying your new pay structure to current employees.
2) For each employee, put in the job title they will have, and all the relevant compensation information.
3) For any employee that you are firing, put in "Terminated" in the "Job Title" column, or "Retired" for any employees who will retire. Then enter "0" for fields with column headers shaded green.
4) Enter the data only in the areas that are shaded grey.
5) Click "Save" to store the new data that you have entered.
6) Click "Retrieve" to restore any data that you have previously saved.
7) Scroll down to see the impact of your decisions in this screen.
8) If you want to restore all the old job titles, click the "Restore Old Job Titles".
9) Once satisfied with your data, click "Next" to move to Screen 3.

| Save | | Retrieve | | Restore Old Job Titles | | Next | | Return |

Emp. #	Emp. Name	Job Title	Pay Grade	New Base Pay Range		Current Base Pay	New Base Pay	Current Ind. Perf. Pay	New Ind. Perf. Pay	Current Grp. Perf. Pay	New Grp. Perf. Pay	Current Org. Perf. Pay	New Org. Perf. Pay	Current Indirect Pay	New Indirect Pay	Current Total Comp.	New Total Comp.
				New Minimum	New Maximum												
1	Affleck, Jen	Secretary				$29,423		$0	$0	$0	$0	$0	$0	$13,147		$42,570	
2	Aurat, Neha	Secretary				$36,667		$0		$0		$0		$16,463		$53,130	
3	Awnashi, Connor	Int Apps Prog - MMS				$44,561		$0		$0		$0		$20,119		$64,680	
4	Berg, Jim	Sr Apps Prog - RS				$63,206		$0		$0		$0		$28,534		$91,740	
5	Boehm, Nick	Jr Apps Prog - MMS				$33,946		$0		$0		$0		$15,004		$48,950	
6	Borycki, Al	Int Apps Prog - MTS				$41,745		$0		$0		$0		$18,755		$60,500	
7	Breitkruz, Lee	Int Apps Prog - SS				$42,504		$0		$0		$0		$19,096		$61,600	
8	Brown, Tracy	Jr Apps Prog - RS				$36,432		$0		$0		$0		$16,368		$52,800	
9	Brucks, Craig	Jr Apps Prog - FMS				$34,914		$0		$0		$0		$15,686		$50,600	
10	Chan, Wing	Sr Apps Prog - FMS				$59,202		$0		$0		$0		$26,598		$85,800	
11	Chau, Yong	Sr Apps Prog - FMS				$57,684		$0		$0		$0		$25,916		$83,600	
12	Chemiske, Amy	Jr Apps Prog - MTS				$37,950		$0		$0		$0		$17,050		$55,000	
13	Chin, Kwok	Int Apps Prog - MMS				$43,263		$0		$0		$0		$19,437		$62,700	
14	Cirkvencic, Cindy	Jr Apps Prog - FMS				$33,726		$0		$0		$0		$15,224		$48,950	
15	Coleman, Trevor	Reg Marketing Mgr				$43,076		$5,500		$0		$0		$21,824		$70,400	
16	Cozac, Terry	Dir Systems Dev				$143,000		$46,750		$0		$0		$63,250		$253,000	
17	Croissant, Dustin	Sys Marketing Spec				$24,552		$6,567		$0		$0		$13,981		$45,100	
18	Currie, Ashton	Jr Apps Prog - RS				$34,914		$0		$0		$0		$15,686		$50,600	
19	Dithavong, Mandu	Sr Apps Prog - MTS				$63,756		$0		$0		$0		$28,644		$92,400	
20	Dorgan, Jolene	Int Apps Prog - RS				$46,299		$0		$0		$0		$20,801		$67,100	

#	Name	Title								
21	Edmondson, Nola	Compensation Clerk	$28,842	$0	$0		$0	$12,958		$41,800
22	Freiheit, Laurel	Sys Marketing Spec	$26,752	$12,716	$0		$0	$17,732		$57,200
23	Gandhi, Jawah	Jr Apps Prog - SS	$33,396	$0	$0		$0	$15,004		$48,400
24	Gargol, Walter	Caretaker	$22,011	$0	$0		$0	$9,889		$31,900
25	Guenther, Michelle	Accountant	$47,058	$0	$0		$0	$21,142		$68,200
26	Hitchings, Ashford	Jr Apps Prog - MMS	$36,432	$0	$0		$0	$16,368		$52,800
27	Jakubiec, Chris E.	Sr Apps Prog - MTS	$60,720	$0	$0		$0	$27,280		$88,000
28	Johns, Jessica	Compensation Clerk	$33,396	$0	$0		$0	$15,004		$48,400
29	Kalra, Suresh	Sr Apps Prog - MMS	$56,166	$0	$0		$0	$25,234		$81,400
30	Kane, Kristie	Dir Human Resources	$115,500	$0	$0		$0	$38,500		$154,000
31	Khosla, Raj	Sys Integration Spec	$67,551	$0	$0		$0	$30,349		$97,900
32	Kumar, Kalburgi	Int Apps Prog - FMS	$44,022	$0	$0		$0	$19,778		$63,800
33	Laing, Patricia	Jr Systems Trainer	$32,258	$0	$0		$0	$14,493		$46,750
34	Leach, Tommy	Sr Sys Install Spec	$55,407	$0	$0		$0	$24,893		$80,300
35	Loblaw, Cora	Sr Apps Prog - SS	$60,720	$0	$0		$0	$27,280		$88,000
36	Ludu, Pradeep	Int Apps Prog - SS	$43,263	$0	$0		$0	$19,437		$62,700
37	Matsalla, Joe D.	Reg Marketing Mgr	$46,684	$11,000	$0		$0	$25,916		$83,600
38	Matshes, Jay	Sr Sys HW Analyst	$59,961	$0	$0		$0	$26,939		$86,900
39	McQueen, Derrick	Jr Apps Prog - SS	$40,986	$0	$0		$0	$18,414		$59,400
40	Miller, Dean	Int Apps Prog - FMS	$41,745	$0	$0		$0	$18,755		$60,500
41	Nesbit, Roger	Sys Integration Spec	$62,238	$0	$0		$0	$27,962		$90,200
42	Paluck, Darren	Sys Marketing Spec	$26,752	$16,522	$0		$0	$19,096		$62,370
43	Pappadanis, Ari	Sr Apps Prog - MMS	$62,238	$0	$0		$0	$27,962		$90,200
44	Rammaya, Anuj	Int Apps Prog - MTS	$47,817	$0	$0		$0	$21,483		$69,300
45	Rans, Scot	Sys Design Analyst	$56,166	$0	$0		$0	$25,234		$81,400
46	Rezansoff, Erin	Compensation Officer	$31,119	$0	$0		$0	$13,981		$45,100
47	Ripley, Thomas	Sr Apps Prog - RS	$56,166	$0	$0		$0	$25,234		$81,400
48	Selensky, Alwyn	Int Apps Prog - RS	$44,022	$0	$0		$0	$19,778		$63,800
49	Shumaker, Gavin	Sys Design Analyst	$50,116	$0	$0		$0	$22,506		$72,622
50	Simpson, Fred	Accountant	$42,504	$0	$0		$0	$19,096		$61,600
51	Sproule, Natalia	Jr Systems Trainer	$33,396	$0	$0		$0	$15,004		$48,400
52	Stadnyk, Darren	Caretaker	$22,770	$0	$0		$0	$10,230		$33,000
53	Stewart, Stephanie	Compensation Mgr	$41,745	$0	$0		$0	$18,755		$60,500
54	Stefaniuk, Michelle	Dir Marketing	$121,000	$11,000	$0		$0	$44,000		$176,000
55	Sundby, Reid	Sys Marketing Spec	$24,552	$8,085	$0		$0	$14,663		$47,300
56	Wapniaski, Stacey	Sr Sys HW Analyst	$61,479	$0	$0		$0	$27,621		$89,100
57	Wong, Alvin	Jr Apps Prog - MTS	$37,950	$0	$0		$0	$17,050		$55,000
58	Wong, Sheldon	Mgr - FMS Dev	$99,550	$0	$0		$0	$33,000		$132,550
59	Wormsbecker, Dan	Sr Sys Install Spec	$57,904	$0	$0		$0	$25,916		$83,820
60	Wu, Tong	Sr Apps Prog - SS	$55,198	$0	$0		$0	$24,552		$79,750
	No. of Emps. on Payroll: 60	COLUMN TOTALS	$2,938,372	$118,140	$0	$0	$0	$1,310,070	$0	$4,366,582

- 106-

Phase III - Screen 3

1) If you are planning to hire any new employees, fill their projected compensation information in the areas shaded grey.

2) Click "Save" to store the information you have entered.

3) Click "Retrieve" to restore any data that you have previously saved in this screen.

4) Click "Next" to go to Screen 4.

| Save | Retrieve | Next | Return |

Emp. #	Emp. Name	Job Title	Pay Grade	Base Pay	Ind. Perf. Pay	Grp. Perf. Pay	Org. Perf. Pay	Indirect Pay	Total Comp.
TOTALS				$0	$0	$0	$0	$0	$0

No. of New Hires: 0

- 107 -

Phase III - Screen 4

1) This screen simply summarizes your recommended compensation budget for the coming year, and compares it to the current year.

2) Review this information and reflect on whether these results will maximize the success of the company.

Return   Finish

RECOMMENDED COMPENSATION BUDGET

Description	No. of Emps.	Base Pay	Ind. Perf. Pay	Grp. Perf. Pay	Org. Perf. Pay	Indirect Pay	Total Comp.
Recommended Compensation Totals (From Screen 2)	60	$0	$0	$0	$0	$0	$0
New Hire Compensation Totals (From Screen 3)	0	$0	$0	$0	$0	$0	$0
Recommended Compensation Budget	60	$0	$0	$0	$0	$0	$0
Current Compensation Totals (From Screen 1)	60	$2,938,372	$118,140	$0	$0	$1,310,070	$4,366,582
Employment Increase/Decrease (Compared to Employee Total in Screen 1)							0.00%
Budget Increase/Decrease (Compared to Current Compensation Totals in Screen 1)							0.00%

Instructions for First Use of CompSoft

1. Insert the CompSoft disc in your CD drive.

2. Click "My Computer."

3. You should then see a file "COMPSOFT(D:)" (if "D" is your CD drive name) in your CD drive. Double click it.

4. You will see three files. Select "CompSoftPhaseII.XLS" and then *either* "CompSoftPhaseIIIDuplox.xls" *or* "CompSoftPhaseIIIZenith.xls", depending on which is your client firm, by clicking "Edit" and then clicking on "Copy to Folder."

5. Go to a directory of your choice. (You may want to create a new folder labelled "Compensation" or something similar.) Click "Copy."

6. You are now done with your disc. You should always work from your hard drive file, not from the disc. Put the disc away for possible use in case you need to re-load the software.

7. Next, go to your folder, open it, and click on the file you want to work with. (At this stage, it will likely be the Phase II file.)

8. The first screen of CompSoft will come up. Accompanying this may be a "Security Warning." If so, click on "Options" and then click "Enable this content."

9. *Do **not** alter the CompSoft file names in any way! Doing so can cause unpredictable consequences with the software, and may cause incorrect calculations or other problems!*